WAR AND CONSCIENCE IN AMERICA

WAR
AND
CONSCIENCE
IN
AMERICA

by Edward LeRoy Long, Jr.

The Westminster Press · Philadelphia

LIBRARY OF CONGRESS CATALOG CARD No. 68–22645

Published by The Westminster Press®
Philadelphia, Pennsylvania

PRINTED IN THE UNITED STATES OF AMERICA .

To my sons
Roger, Charles, and Douglas

PREFACE

My awareness of the need for this book was made clear to me when I conducted a seminar on this subject at Oberlin College. No small credit is deserved by the members of that seminar for exciting my further explorations into the issues that it uncovered. The process continued while I was teaching in the summer session at Union Theological Seminary in New York City.

In the early stages of writing, Prof. Ralph Potter, of Harvard University, prodded and inspired me to finish as quickly as I could. Several individuals, including students, read a penultimate version. Among those whose helpful comments I must particularly acknowledge are the Reverend William Cook, National Field Director of the Council on Religion and International Affairs; Dr. Alan Geyer, Director of International Relations, Council for Christian Social Action, United Church of Christ; Dr. Roger Shinn, William Dodge Professor of Applied Christianity at Union Theological Seminary; and Dr. H. Thomas Frank, an Oberlin colleague. While it is always true that an author must take responsibility for the final product, it is especially necessary in this case. The comments of these men were helpful in no small measure because their approach to these problems comes out of a stance somewhat different from my own.

E. L. L., Jr.

Oberlin, Ohio

CONTENTS

INTRODUCTION

On a Sunday morning in the fall of 1967 an otherwise little known Episcopal rector created a national stir by interrupting a sermon and asking the President of the United States, who was worshiping in his congregation, to give "some logical, straightforward explanation" for the involvement of the United States in the Vietnam war. The news wires buzzed. The rector was criticized by some for "exquisite bad taste"; he was defended by others for voicing a profound public hunger for a greater understanding of national policy.

At almost the same time a group of clergymen at a national conference on the church and society, acting as individuals, called on young men to resist the draft by means of civil disobedience. Declaring the war in Vietnam "unjust," these clergymen, including many in the ecclesiastical "establishment" of their day, were implying a need for the Christian church to make an "all-out" protest against national policy, even to the point of disobeying laws.

A few days after his visit to the church the President answered the rector by saying at a news conference, "Our aims in Vietnam have been very clear from the beginning." He mused to the effect that "even all

the preachers in the country had heard about [them]."
He might have turned the tables and asked the preachers for "some logical, straightforward explanation" of
their criteria for judging the recent military operations
of our country to be "unjust." If the rector was right
in demanding a logically compelling justification in
political terms for our involvement in Southeast Asia,
would not the President have been right in demanding
a logically compelling explanation in moral terms for
a policy of dissent and disobedience?

These two incidents are but isolated events in a
continuing debate that has been marked by perplexity
and attended by turmoil. People on both sides have
been more adamant in their convictions than articulate
in their reasoning. They appeal to moral premises without engaging in moral reasoning. Although each group
sometimes asks the other for explanation, more often
one badgers the other with slogans, epithets, picket
signs, or implications of bad faith.

The political and moral assumptions guiding
twenty years or more of opposition to international
Communism no longer receive unquestioned support.
A generation that experienced Communism as a great
international threat managed by military control from
one center is now becoming old and even passing away.
In some cases even its representatives have come to
question the perpetual efficacy of a policy of containment based upon a professed willingness to shower
"massive retaliation" against any Communist country
engaged in expansion by coercion. Moreover, as a
younger generation knows, the policy of containment
has not been entirely effective, the Communist world
is no longer a simple monolith, and the last fifteen years

have been given over to extinguishing small fires on the periphery of great conflict areas rather than holding inflexible lines in an international *status quo* composed of only two great power blocs.

What is even more striking is the extent to which the contemporary debate has moved from considerations of policy alone to a renewed appeal to conscience and moral criteria. The situation breaks upon us following a long period in which some churches have simply desired to provide a spiritual sanctuary above the enigmas and evils of the world. And many others, even in understandable efforts to be politically relevant, have failed to engage in a sustained explanation of the moral implications of either participation in war or conscientious objection to war. The resulting motivational turmoil is enormous and racks the spirit of the country. Young men of military age are frequently faced with decisions about these matters without ever having heard them discussed in schools, churches, or synagogues. Silence in public schools is understandable; in the churches, inexcusable.

This volume is written to help all of us to think more searchingly about the agonizing problems raised by war—and about the moral issues confronting young men who face military service. The issues explored are heightened but not exhausted by a particular conflict. Wars of insurgency fought under jungle conditions in underdeveloped nations raise the moral problems of war in new forms. Many regard such conditions as rendering military enterprises so destructive of civil order as to make them both repugnant and indefensible.

While the discussion does not ignore questions of political consequence, it directs attention mainly to the problems of individual conscience in confronting alternatives of judgment, decision, and opinion, as well as alternatives of action, available under national policy. With respect to the moral issues its purpose is more to examine than to advocate, more to explain than to exhort. It ends, however, with a plea for the nation to expand the freedom available to men of many convictions so that they may all relate constructively to the needs of these times and to one another in the midst of rending diversities.

The appeals for individual moral authenticity which have arisen in our time have not always been couched in the traditional idiom of Christian faith. Some readers may wish to translate what is written here to the language of another world view. But regardless of the language, the problems to be faced and the decisions to be made will not be fundamentally different from, or less difficult than, those confronting the Christian conscience. Every sensitive individual must make his own conscientious response to these matters in the light of that which makes the most authentic claims upon his loyalties.

I. THE CHANGING NATURE OF WAR

The news broadcast finished with its daily account of the fighting. The story this time was about the evacuation of an entire village and its subsequent destruction. All the inhabitants had been ordered at gunpoint to pack within thirty minutes for transport to a refugee center. As the last helicopter lifted off the ground, demolition was begun and the town reduced to rubble.

A veteran of the Second World War sighed: "When I fought we did not destroy towns like that. We only searched out the snipers and rounded up the collaborators. We left the village to serve the needs of simple people who could do us no harm."

"But war is different now," retorted his son, fresh home from basic training. "We must destroy whole towns in order to secure an area. In guerrilla warfare the insurgents infiltrate everything. Moreover, you cannot tell who is a member of the opposition and who is loyal to your side. To leave anything to chance is to threaten the safety of the entire area."

This conversation illustrates the moral perplexity that plagues a nation engaged in a new type of war. Those responsible for the fighting seem driven by the realities of circumstance to justify horrendous strategies to win against a fluid, treacherous, and persistent foe. Those accustomed to the restraints of civilization, even in the conduct of war, are revolted by the measures that seem necessary to deal with such realities. They are impelled to question the legitimacy of warfare when its very pursuit seems to demand the disregard of so many human sensitivities.

"We must protect peoples from aggression," runs a common defense of our role in Southeast Asia. The moral principle to which this appeals has been honored by civilized men since the advent of ethical reflection. The actions by which it is implemented are now, like napalm, intensified and frightening.

"We are fighting an unjust war," runs the countercharge. The situation referred to is as fresh as the morning newspaper. The category for evaluating it is as old as Christendom.

Each new war poses old moral issues in new ways. The soldier in Vietnam uses entirely different weapons,

2

has been trained under quite different conditions, and thinks of his task with different imagery than did the medieval knight on a crusade in the Holy Land. But he may employ some of the same moral reasoning in defense of what he is doing as did his counterpart in shining armor. Similarly, today's conscientious objector in alternative civilian service relates very differently to his nation than did a persecuted early Christian, but his decision to refuse the use of the sword may rest on the same reasoning as that used in apostolic times.

Several factors have given modern war its present character. Nations today do not submit their actions to scrutiny by a higher political or moral authority. Neither the United Nations nor the combined voices of several church bodies seem able to deter nations determined to pursue policies they believe to be in their self-interest. War today is fought with weapons whose destructive efficiency staggers the imaginations even of those who have been reared on science fiction and comic strips. Field combat today is crude, ugly, and gruesome, and may well be more gory than anything known in the past. Finally, within recent years we have seen gross violations of the international rules of war— torture, brainwashing of prisoners, and disregard for the traditional procedures and rules of military conflict. War is now a technically escalated primitivism that casts every moral issue into bold relief.

THE IMPACT OF NATIONAL SOVEREIGNTY

Modern war is waged by the nation-state, either independently or in consort with other nation-states. The nation-state possesses the right and power to wage war and no analysis of the conditions and morality of modern warfare can ignore this sovereignty. Its consequences are legion both for the making of policy and for the emotional loyalties associated with the military enterprise.

In thinking about political responsibilities, leaders and moralists alike must proceed as citizens of nation-states. Americans must ask themselves about their task as Americans; Englishmen, about their task as Englishmen. Even those alliances formed by nations of a common purpose hark back for their significance to the sovereignty of the powers that constitute them. Institutes of defense analysis ("think tanks") are usually wedded to a concept of national self-interest and seek to be responsible within that framework. They know they cannot change or alter the present control of military power by individual nation-states and hence defend the touchstone of national self-interest as relevant both to the current situation and to the wider interests of mankind.

For many individuals who think about war as a problem of conscience the emotional loyalties engendered by the love of country are probably more decisive. When men say, "My country, right or wrong," they usually have in mind its military exploits rather than its tax policy or welfare programs! The love of country has the same power to attract unqualified support for armed conflict today as the appeal for the defense of Christendom had in the times of the Crusades. There is an inevitably monogamous relationship between patriotic ceremonies and military symbolism.

We decry this when we see it manifested in the

thinking and behavior of other nations. Our indignation is kindled when we find them singing *"Deutschland über Alles"* or refusing to submit to the world community. But this kindled wrath betrays our own presumption of righteousness and our willingness to condemn others more readily than we criticize ourselves. In the First World War we believed atrocity stories about Germany that were later shown to be unfounded. We could do this because the enemy was "another kind of nation." Of "another" against whom we fight it is possible to believe anything, particularly reports that serve to reinforce moral outrage.

Atrocity stories about enemies have long ceased to be figments only of the nationalistic imagination. Nazi behavior in the Second World War exceeded the worst fabricated portrayals of the First World War. Treatment of political enemies has demonstrated that cruelty can be a commonplace. Paradoxically we have often responded with less self-righteousness to the real situations than we did to imagined ones.

Both the imagined atrocity story and the actual atrocities stem from much the same source. The one stems from a patriotic self-righteousness that engenders such contempt for another nation as to regard it as capable of any degree of moral depravity. The other arises when regimes of state acknowledge no requirement of moral decency and no standards of humane behavior as binding upon their actions. Both are instances of nationalism or its ideological equivalent.

The role of the nation-state crucially shapes the moral judgments made of wartime actions. A case study in point is saturation bombing, which came to be used extensively in the Second World War by the very Allied nations that had strong initial scruples about its legitimacy.

In 1937 Franco's forces attacked a Spanish town of Guernica from the air and killed many unarmed civilians. In the same year the Japanese bombed Nanking. The Government of the United States protested the Japanese action by declaring, "This Government holds the view that any general bombing of an extensive area wherein there resides a large populace engaged in peaceful pursuits is unwarranted and contrary to the principles of law and humanity."[1] In the early stages of the Second World War, President Roosevelt called for restraint on the practice of obliteration bombing and declared that air attacks upon helpless civilians were morally unacceptable.

It was the inner logic of war and not a deliberate change in moral ideals that eroded the resolve not to bomb targets whose destruction also entailed the annihilation of civilians. Even though the German air force first expanded this practice at Warsaw, Rotterdam, and Coventry, the United States and Britain did not strike back merely in a moral effort to "punish" such conduct. Policy was altered as a consequence of other factors.

The Allies began by bombing military targets with precision methods that largely spared civilians. But they soon discovered that daytime raids, in which precision was possible, were very dangerous. Nighttime raids were safer but less precise. The Royal Air Force, which had suffered painful losses with early daylight raids, went to nighttime bombing while the United

States Eighth Air Force conducted precision daytime raids. Both Allies came to support the practice of mass bombing of the very sort that had earlier received unqualified condemnation by American political leaders. An article by Vera Brittain attacking this "Massacre by Bombing" met very hostile public response in March, 1944.

Military considerations also led to a change of moral outlook in the fighting against Japan. Our bombing of Japan began with high-altitude precision bombing, but General LeMay concluded that this tactic was not yielding adequate results. He devised the massive incendiary raid against a whole city. These raids were justified by the argument that the productive capacity of Japan was scattered throughout its cities, making it necessary to attack civilians in order to knock out war factories. This change of tactics was defended because it helped the right nation to win the war.

In addition to the criticism from Miss Brittain, one Roman Catholic just war theorist criticized these shifts of strategy as morally intolerable, but the officials responsible stood ready to defend the bombing and the general public was obviously prepared to condone it. Obliteration bombing came to be accepted because strategic necessity combined with national self-interest to make it useful. Moral evaluations called into question neither factor. We have been living with this legacy ever since.

These transformations in our conception of tolerable practice took place before the discovery and manufacture of the atomic bomb. They contributed to what Robert C. Batchelder has called "the Irreversible

Decision" to use that bomb in the massive destruction of two cities. Speaking of that decision, Batchelder has concluded:

> The assumptions that war is primarily a military matter, that war is now total, that the purpose of fighting a war is to achieve military victory, and that war can end in victory only if the enemy is forced to surrender unconditionally—these came to be accepted as self-evident and unquestionable truths by the vast majority of the American people, despite the fact that such axioms stand in direct contradiction to the main stream of Christian ethical thought about war. Such general assumptions about modern war were at least as important—if not more so—in the shaping of the decision to drop the atomic bomb as were the ethical considerations consciously brought to bear upon that particular choice. What is required for the future is not only that proper ethical thinking be applied to the making of each particular policy decision affecting nuclear weapons. It is even more important that our whole style of thinking about war be such that these particular decisions are not—as in 1945—morally compromised before they are reached.[2]

ATOMIC AND NUCLEAR WEAPONS

The mushroom clouds that rose over two Japanese cities in 1945 have become symbols of a larger complex of technical developments affecting the making of war. Much discussion has taken place concerning Christian imperatives in an era of seemingly ultimate weapons. This discussion has usually occurred on the assumption that the use of such weapons will be decisively significant in *any* outbreak of future hostilities. This assumption has proven, temporarily at least, mis-

8

taken. Since the advent of such weapons several international conflicts have been fought with conventional methods. However, there is always the possibility that issues examined on the assumption that war will entail the use of such devices may arise. The nuclear stalemate cannot be taken for granted despite its persistence for more than two decades of cold war tension.

The possession of nuclear weapons has been a political factor in an international order held together in part by the deterrent effect of balanced terror. The resulting "peace" seems successful because the major powers in possession of such threats have not actually used them. Meanwhile, atomic and nuclear stockpiles have not diminished despite efforts made to agree about bans upon their use.

We can be soberly grateful because political events have managed to transpire without prompting the use of atomic and nuclear weapons as instruments of military action. But we cannot take this as a sign that the moral questions involved in the possession and threatened use of these weapons have been solved.

Throughout a long debate on this matter men have analyzed the issues posed by atomic weapons with the use of the same categories that have been unsuccessful for resolving the question of war in general. One group has argued that the advent of nuclear weapons means that war must be forsworn completely. This judgment has come most easily for pacifists, since it represents the extension of their convictions to a new situation. Armed with evidence of the potentially suicidal destruction that can be expected in a nuclear conflagration, the pacifists have believed that idealistic and pragmatic considerations now coalesce to demand

9

the abolition of all war. In some cases they have pleaded for nonviolence and in other cases for international law as a feasible means of resisting evil in the international arena, but in either case they have declared that "any society willing to commit such total destruction [as that entailed in the use of nuclear weapons] is in utter revolt against God's purposes in the creation, preservation and redemption of mankind."[3]

Others, including many nonpacifists, have judged that the use of nuclear weapons should be forsworn in advance. Noting the close relationship between obliteration bombing and nuclear weapons, these conclude, along with Helmut Gollwitzer, that "with such weapons it is impossible to conduct a war for the defense of justice, as in former times. They are only suitable for a war which tramples all justice and humanity underfoot."[4]

The Second Vatican Council wrestled at great length with this issue in the light of traditional Roman Catholic teaching about war. There was strong sentiment in favor of declaring that the use of nuclear weapons entails a degree of destruction that exceeds all reasonable proportion and must therefore be judged as wicked. The final declaration first mentions the multiplication of scientific weapons that "can inflict massive and indiscriminate destruction far exceeding the bounds of legitimate defense," and then declares: "Any act of war aimed indiscriminately at the destruction of entire cities or of extensive areas along with their population is a crime against God and man himself. It merits unequivocal and unhesitating condemnation."[5]

Some of those who have concurred in the argument that the use of nuclear weapons for obliteration bombing in a future war can never be justified have, however, found themselves unprepared to abandon nuclear deterrence. They have tried to reject the use of the nuclear bomb for the future while accepting the continued possession of the weapon as a temporary means of balancing the power of other nations in a position to blackmail the world with it. The difficulty involved in trying to possess the bomb as a deterrent while doubting the moral validity of its use in any future conflict has been frankly acknowledged by John C. Bennett:

> It would be less than candid if I did not admit a real difficulty that I feel. . . . If the points that I shall now make should be greatly emphasized in our country, the effect might be some lessening of the power and the capacity for maneuver of the United States and other nations which are seeking to balance the power of the Communist nations. One could feel less inner conflict about this matter if there were in the Soviet Union and China freedom for this kind of utterance. I believe, however, that those who share the views which I shall present should not keep silent even though what they say may have some undesired effects. We are dealing with a dilemma. If we cover up the depth of the problem on one side of this dilemma, there is certain to be a measure of blindness to this side of our policy.[6]

Herman Kahn has challenged the legitimacy or possibility of maintaining such a "bluff" with nuclear deterrence. Writing from assumptions, often shared by political analysts, that modern man has ceased to permit moral considerations to enter into military de-

11

cisions, Kahn has concluded that a strategy of "bluff deterrence" is politically impossible to carry off—at least in a free society. Military planning must accept the fact that any premature abdication of thermonuclear defense can only invite destructive consequences for all that Americans hold dear. We must, he has argued, accept the legitimacy of planning for a nuclear conflict and make serious plans for partial survival. Only by doing so can we make a potential enemy take our possession of nuclear weapons as a serious deterrent.[7]

Yet another line of reasoning finds nuclear weapons to be morally unacceptable only if used in massive obliteration bombing or the threatened use of such bombing. If nuclear power can be harnessed to strategic devices aimed with discrimination at military targets, it raises no new moral problems. This is the burden of Paul Ramsey's observation that "counterforce nuclear war is the upper limit of rational, politically purposive military action."[8] Rather than outdating war on moral grounds, nuclear weapons of this sort become important aspects of the balance of power that deters men from unjust aggression.

With the advent of land wars in underdeveloped parts of the world our frustration is heightened by our possession of nuclear weapons. Not only do these weapons fail to resolve the moral problems, they complicate our political resolves. We have frequently hoped that threats of "massive retaliation" would preserve peace by making aggressors think twice before overrunning others. Instead, they have driven others to erode peace through little campaigns that are never massive enough to be answered massively. The torturous choice involved in the morality of war persists with new complications. We have to limit ourselves in practice to conventional means of warfare that are ugly, dirty, and discouraging and in which our technical superiority is rendered impotent by moral reservations we cannot in good conscience ignore.

An Instance of Limited War

The conflict in Korea was the first international dispute of the nuclear age to involve the United States in a major use of military power. The memories of the Second World War were vivid and the fear of nuclear warfare strong. Hope for the success of the United Nations—still in its infancy—ran high. International Communism was assumed to be expansionist by definition and the tensions and lines of the cold war were drawn with clarity under the Truman Doctrine. The United States was prepared to fight a war, but only providing it did not get too big. There was no mood to mobilize for total conflict such as marked the Allied cause in the two world wars.

There was, of course, intense debate about the Korean conflict. The debate arose from the discontent in several segments of American society with the limitations inherent in pursuing police action in consort with other members of the United Nations. These critics detested President Truman's steadfast refusal to permit the conflict to escalate into a war that might entail a land conflict with China or the use of atomic weapons.

13

They called it "Truman's Folly" and "the war we didn't fight to win." They hailed it as the salvation of the United Nations and the turning point in the struggle against Communist expansion, damned it as "the mess in Korea," and made it the most overworked and unsettled issue in the repertoire of parlor orators. It was the most disheartening and frustrating, the coldest and dreariest, the least inspiring and least popular war in American history. Yet it was, for the United States and its United Nations allies, an effort of high purpose and the most selfless idealism, earnestly dedicated to the preservation of peace and freedom.[9]

The Korean conflict brought new dimensions to international conflict. It was frequently referred to as "police action," partly because it was a joint undertaking with the United Nations and partly because military strategy was deliberately limited by political considerations. The symbol of this perplexity and frustration was the policy disagreement that arose between President Truman and General MacArthur over the proper response that should be made to the entry of Chinese troops into the conflict. General MacArthur, standing in a long tradition of American military thinking, offered the Chinese a battlefield truce, but threatened to extend the bounds of the conflict if his offer was rejected. President Truman, having decided to hold hostilities to those acts necessary to protect that portion of Korea lying south of the 38th parallel, and sensing the policy disagreements between himself and MacArthur, relieved one of the most popularly illustrious generals in recent American history of his command.

This action struck directly at a psychology of war

that has been part of American attitudes for decades. Traditionally we have fought to win—decisively, quickly, and without deference to the cautious sensitivities of international bodies. We see ourselves as destined to punish, not merely to stop, aggression—to destroy a nation that offends international law, not merely to make it retreat to the line from which it embarks on aggression. A nation of zealots might not have accepted the Truman action had not the fear of nuclear warfare hung like a sword of Damocles over the world. There was no mood for a global confrontation with the other side even though there was little in the way of supportive understanding for a limited war in the thinking of the American public. While zealous patriots anguished about a "war we could not win," they were unable to make a nation adopt an all-out policy. A President with a strong will, stubbornly dedicated to his duty as he read it, could withstand the pressures upon him to escalate the conflict because the public mood was tacitly on his side.

The restraints shown by American policy reflected a sensitivity to world opinion as expressed through the United Nations. This exerted a pressure against rash actions that was probably as crucial as was the caution and prudence in the mood at home. In June, 1952, five hundred American planes bombed Communist power plants in North Korea. The British House of Commons reacted with the demand that American direction over policy in the war be more carefully scrutinized and, if necessary, qualified. Despite the disadvantages to quick military responses entailed in the review of our actions by other members of an international body, this was one factor in creating a new kind of war.

No national crisis can be weathered without observations from preachers and theological journalists. Pulpits and magazines commented upon the war in Korea, often to express the hope that the conflict would not turn into a nuclear war. In the main the action in Korea was accepted as an extension of the policy justified by the logic of the Second World War and by Communist expansion in Eastern Europe and China. There was little resurgent isolationism. The United States was understood as taking positive responsibility in an international crisis. Indeed it was even better than this, for due cooperation with the United Nations was being achieved. The United Nations was consulted, included, and even nominally charged with the direction of policy. We implemented its wishes. Policy planners in the Department of Defense went along with the moral distinctions between military action on an unlimited scale and the kind of "policing" being done in Korea. The State Department was aware that major reconstruction through political/economic programs should follow the military phase of the undertaking and even Congress was voting funds for international relief and rehabilitation. All of this most religious commentators accepted as healthy.

But not all Christians were happy. Alfred Hassler, presumably reflecting a large segment of pacifist feeling, expressed serious disagreement with the policy and its premises. He realized that many Americans supported the action in Korea, including a number of pacifists who might be opposed to a strident military policy. But, he demurred:

16

Whatever the technical definitions—and however blinded the pacifists—practically, the fighting in Korea is indistinguishable from war. Two armies are struggling against each other. Each is killing as many of the other's personnel as it can. Each has recourse to all the weapons of war it has available, and has no hesitation about bombing and strafing roads, railroads, villages and noncombatants where such action seems to its immediate advantage. And, of course, men are being killed on just as wholesale a scale as if the action were openly labeled war.[10]

In spite of the MacArthurs and the Hasslers the Korean war was fought to a negotiated stalemate. It was unpopular but not widely denounced on moral grounds. It was ended through the efforts of a military hero who could do what no pacifists could ever do—persuade a nation to accept a solution without victory as a viable form of national self-interest. The "proto-hawks" of Korean days were rendered politically ineffective by the accidental fact that public support turned to a general acting the role of a "proto-dove." Once the conflict was smothered the public became understandably content to forget the moral and policy issues involved or else to let a few historians debate the matter in scholarly analyses. Even the bellicists ceased to fume about a "no win" policy, at least until new hostilities in Asia subsequently appeared.

INSURGENCY WARFARE: A POLICY DILEMMA

It was the cherished hope of many that, as Robert T. Oliver put it, "Korea will stand in the annals of the twentieth century as the place in which Communism was finally halted and turned back in Asia."[11]

Such hopes, however, have proven illusory. Some say we "did not lick them"; others, that we failed to capitalize upon a favorable military situation with broad programs of political wisdom; still others, that the whole nature of the Asian situation has been radically transformed by the rise of nationalistic aspirations only incidentally tied to the dynamics of Communism.

Certainly not in the memory of any living citizen has it been as difficult to read the implications of political events. Some, like Dean Rusk, are firmly convinced that the situation in Vietnam is basically a new form of attempted Communist expansion, appearing as overt aggression against a nation we have pledged to defend. Others believe that the situation in Vietnam has arisen through that age-old process by which outcasts get under the skin of "in" powers. They reject the mind-set by which the insurgency warfare of this conflict is understood in terms of the model of aggression which applied even to the Korean situation. In that situation the enemy was identifiable, came from the other side of a battle line, and could be driven back to a point of initial aggression. The battle was cold and dirty, plagued by hardship and sacrifice, but not complicated by the confusions and difficulties that arise when friend and foe live side by side in the same territory, look, dress, and speak alike, and can change strategic roles as conditions permit.

The debate that has arisen concerning American policy in Vietnam evidences the perplexity of a nation confronting an insurgent war complicated by intervention on both sides. It also brings new challenges to all the categories through which we have dealt with the problem of war for decades. The fervor is high on all

18

sides of a debate in which the insights are few and the guidelines faint. We should begin to realize the military, political, and moral rethinking that must be done as the precondition for a wise response to this new phenomenon. Meanwhile, segments of the population, emotionally racked by the heavy burden of the moral perplexities, have even ceased to trust in the efficacy of analysis and have moved from the classroom to the streets!

America's youthful exuberance and relative independence from entanglements with the rest of the world have generally permitted us to find simple justifications for our causes. When practically the whole nation agrees about the moral legitimacy of a particular policy, as it has in all the major wars of this century, statesmen do not become adept in dealing with inherent moral dilemmas. Even moralists learn to oversimplify.

The moral problems occasioned by our involvement in Vietnam have not suddenly granted us the depth maturity with which alone we can understand them. Nor does it seem to make any difference whether those who analyze the war do so from a perspective of political hardheadedness and national self-interest or from the perspectives of a Christian morality. Men of equal wisdom and commensurate dedication come to profoundly divergent conclusions which they hold with equal tenacity. James Finn was not far from the mark when he declared, "Our public debate is, if not a shambles, a disgrace."[12] A bitter polarization about fundamental national purpose creates an experience that, while not unprecedented in less crucial pasts, is new to most of us.

If we are to raise the level of our national debate, whether between a father and his draftee son or between a Secretary of State and a chairman of the Senate Foreign Relations Committee, we must become better informed, not only concerning political realities but about the moral categories with which we assess them. The debates today refer to terms such as "just" and "unjust" war. These terms have significant historical roots and meanings and cannot be employed for the equivalent of "approve" or "disapprove." If some men are called by conscience to reject war in general, or this war in particular, they should stand well informed about the ground upon which other men in other times have made similar decisions. War creates both problems of policy and problems of conscience. Thinking about both deserves the resources of a well-furbished awareness of historic Christian teaching concerning grounds for both participation in, and objection to, armed conflict.

II. RELIGIOUS SUPPORT FOR CONSCIENTIOUS PARTICIPATION

Returning from a trip to Vietnam as one of twenty-two observers sent by the President, Archbishop R. E. Lucey, of San Antonio, was direct and blunt. "It is necessary to use force," he said in a statement for the press, "and the man who doesn't believe in force will soon be a slave. You cannot have peace in the world without force because there are evil men in the world."[1]

The archbishop was but one of that majority of Christians who have found it both possible and imperative to support war as an act of conscience.

Throughout most of Western history Christians have taken up the sword, sometimes in unquestioning allegiance to a prince or to a nation, but more frequently as a response to keenly felt moral obligation. Some have made statements for newspapers; others have put their reasoning into careful treatises justifying their position. Theological world views of widespread intellectual significance have developed as responses to the necessity of combating evil and injustice in the world through military means.

The resultant thinking has developed along three main lines, each of which has been advocated with great care and defended with remarkable thoroughness by Christian thinkers. While not completely exclusive of one another, these positions find very different moral meanings in the same political actions and should be set forth independently.

Christian Teaching About the Just War

For three centuries the Christian movement had existed as a persecuted minority, given no status by, and indebted for no duties to, the civil order. Constantine reversed the policy of the Empire and made Christianity, at first a tolerated and in time, the official religion of the political realm. Christians realized that their relationship to the state was altered. They could no longer ignore the requirement of citizenship and accepted an obligation to maintain justice as a social good. They also acknowledged that the Empire of which they were a part maintained itself by warding off barbarians through the use of military force.

22

The result of this shift in circumstances was a sobered and tempered sense of Christian responsibility for the structures of society that were sustained internally and defended externally by coercive means. They believed that these structures of justice had been instituted by God, but they also recognized that they were maintained in practical political life by the use of arms. Augustine was aware that the justice maintained by men in this fashion was a human and imperfect achievement, attended by misery and suspicion. But he saw the alternative to be lawlessness, and argued that the benefits of even a forced unity were preferable to the miseries that would flow from a Christian refusal to protect the Empire from subversion within and from conquest and destruction without. Hence he concluded:

The wise man will wage just wars. . . . [But he will also] lament the necessity of just wars, if he remembers that he is a man; for if they were not just he would not wage them, and would therefore be delivered from all wars. For it is the wrong-doing of the opposing party which compels the wise man to wage just wars; this wrong-doing, even though it gave rise to no war, would still be matter of grief to man because it is man's wrong-doing. Let every one, then, who thinks with pain on all these great evils, so horrible, so ruthless, acknowledge that this is misery. And if any one either endures or thinks of them without mental pain, this is a more miserable plight still, for he thinks himself happy because he has lost human feeling.[2]

The moralists and theologians who have developed the doctrine of a just war have carefully specified the conditions under which the use of armed coercion can be defended. They have concluded both that the cause for which military action is undertaken must be morally legitimate and that the means by which victory is sought must be kept under ethical scrutiny. They have enunciated various criteria for judging both the goals sought by and the means used in a just war. No particular way of stating these conditions has been officially codified, but the same criteria appear among different theologians with sufficient regularity to provide the following principles.

a. *All other means to the morally just solution of a conflict must be exhausted before resort to arms can be regarded as legitimate.* A just war must be a last resort, to be accepted only after all reasonable attempts at the reconciliation of issues have failed to bring about a morally tolerable situation. When just war theorists say that all other means to the solution of an issue must be exhausted before the use of arms is legitimate, they have in mind a definite moral line between those means which settle conflicts on the basis of justice and those actions which merely avoid conflict by abdicating moral responsibility. While stressing the obligation to employ peaceful methods for settling disputes, they also stress the importance of bringing such disputes to a morally legitimate conclusion. If necessary, they will fight rather than surrender.

b. *War can be just only if employed to defend a stable order or morally preferable cause against threats of destruction or the rise of injustice.* A just war cannot be fought for unjustifiable goals. Political aggrandizement, selfish acquisitions of either power or wealth, and subversion against social order are ruled

24

out. Military involvements are justified only if they further constructive political and social purposes.

It is easy to oversimplify this criterion. Some Christians have done so by teaching that any rebellion against existing order is unjustified regardless of oppression suffered. More recently, Americans have regarded initial overt military action as the main sign of unjust intentions and argued that a nation must wait to respond until an aggressor makes some move.

Classical thinkers have been more subtle in their analysis. Colonial preachers during the American revolution came to see that even the overthrow of existing authority is justified if a regime persists in denying to its subjects life, liberty, and the pursuit of happiness. Thomas Aquinas, in speaking of these problems, put the matter in a way that emphasizes the moral intentions of an enemy and not merely his overt acts. He wrote, "Those attacked must have, by a fault, deserved to be attacked."[3]

The crucial test in both these instances is a solid measure of justice. If a ruler subverts justice, he is to be overthrown; if a nation dishonors the rights of other nations, it must be sanctioned. Christians may even take initial military action if faced with sufficiently severe provocation.

In theory at least, it might seem that only one side of a conflict could be morally right and hence only one side legitimately able to say that it was justly involved in a war. But war arises precisely because men argue about moral issues. If both sides to a conflict accepted a common and objectivized measure of the moral right, the very root of conflict would be eradicated. Wars occur in situations where there is a dis-

25

agreement about moral justice and hence can take place between two parties each of which claims justice for its cause.

Augustine's thinking about Christian participation in war showed a profound sensitivity to this enigma. He understood how the use of arms was brought about by a contest between relative forms of justice. No completely righteous cause is likely to be found in human partisanships. The Christian cannot expect his cause to be universally regarded as completely right, that of his opponent as totally wrong. Instead, in opposing the wrongdoing of another party, the Christian should be deeply troubled by the unfortunate and tragic consequences of his own actions. Even while defending what he believes to be a good (a good that would be destroyed if he took no action), the Christian understands that he is not making a full victory for righteousness. Since this is the case, he participates in war only with an attitude of humility and repentance, troubled by the misery and the plight of man revealed by the necessity of defending justice with coercive means.

Orators at Veterans Day exercises seldom ask a nation to bewail the past defense of its own liberty. Armchair moralists often declare, "Of course, everyone has a right to protect himself and nations should feel no scruples in fighting for their own survival." But thoughtful Christian teaching about the just war does not accord such unqualified standing to self-defense. Instead, it sees that the protection of the weak or defenseless neighbor from aggression or tyranny has an even prior moral claim. The highest service of justice and order is directed to the protection of others rather than the self, to the preservation of justice and order for all men and not merely to the safeguarding of privileges for some.

c. *A third criterion of the just war specifies that such a war must be carried out with the right attitudes.* Those who resort to violence as an act of justice should avoid vindictive anger and malicious revenge. As Augustine put it, "The desire for harming, the cruelty of avenging, an unruly and implacable animosity, the rage of rebellion, the lust of domination and the like— these are the things which are to be blamed [i.e., considered wrong] in war."[4]

Military actions undertaken as acts of justice should correct some wrong or achieve some protection for righteousness and order. Any goal other than the intention to attain or restore a just and durable peace, whether it takes the form of political imperialism or the intention to visit retaliation on an enemy, cannot sustain the burden of proof for making a particular war just. Slogans like "Remember Pearl Harbor," whatever their value in sustaining the enthusiasm of a nation to fight a treacherous foe, cannot be reconciled with this measure of a just war. The seemingly uninspired statement of a field soldier in Vietnam, "I'm fighting to stay alive, to do my year, and get back home," may be more defensible than the oratory of a morale officer who seeks to whip up hatred of the Vietcong.

d. *A just war must be explicitly declared by a legitimate authority.* A formal declaration of war serves notice between parties that a nation intends to use war as an instrument of political policy. It precludes *sub rosa* military action in which one side stabs

27

another in the back before making its intentions clear and explicit. Many traditional just war theorists have even insisted that a formal declaration of war be preceded by warnings that such an action may be forthcoming so that an offending party has the opportunity to desist in its threat to stability and peace before being declared subject to the possibility of attack.

Only the highest policy body can make the necessary commitment involved in a declaration of war. In the past this has meant the ruling prince; today it generally means a duly constituted authority of the nation-state. Only the political leader or policy-making body that ensures the common defense has access to diplomatic information and influence, and can marshal the great majority of the citizens into a common endeavor is in a position to relate military operations to political purposes. Individual Christians or small groups that take up arms for pet desires cannot justify their actions in terms of structural justice and legal process.

e. *A just war may be conducted only by military means that promise a reasonable attainment of the moral and political objectives being sought.* The measure of a just war is sometimes phrased by saying that a particular engagement must "have a reasonable chance of success." People jump to the conclusion that Christians may resort to war only if they can be on the winning side, but something more profound is at stake. Any victory attained by military means must leave what is defended in reasonable tact and must offer constructive political and social consequences. If there are no prospects for a constructive outcome from a military venture, if the use of arms can result only in the utter destruction and annihilation of those structures of justice and human communities which the resort to arms is designed to protect—then the war is unjust and morally wrong because it is practically futile.

A just war must employ means that may be expected to bring constructive results proportional to the evil required to attain them. This principle of proportion is not simple, for the task of weighing military destruction against moral and political advantages is difficult. But all military operations must be scrutinized by a test which weighs costs against consequences. A military commander would be morally wrong in conducting operations at great loss of life if they did not yield strategic advantages. Similarly, damage to an enemy cannot be sanctioned if it entails more destruction than is required to force his surrender.

The just war heritage keeps prudential factors prominent over emotional and ideological considerations. War cannot be just if used by a nation to express its hostility, vent its emotions, display its heroism, or commit its own suicide in order to remain faithful to an abstract ideal. Men are not to be sacrificed for symbolic reasons or to attain victories that yield only emotional satisfactions. Grave consequences alone can justify grave actions.

f. *The just war theory has also entailed selective immunity for certain parts of the population, particularly for noncombatants.* Civilians should be spared from such blatantly hostile acts as wanton destruction, looting of homes, pilferage of goods, forced involvement in military operations. Civilians are not to be impressed into the direct military service of a conquering party—though of course once the territory in which they live has been occupied they can be required to submit to the rule of the conquering forces. Direct attacks upon noncombatants, vindictive torture of residents in occupied areas, etc., would clearly violate the canons of just war.

While ideally, just war theorists have ruled as unjust any taking of civilian or noncombatant lives, they have always conceded that civilian casualties sometimes occur as the side effect of a military operation. When a military target—a fair object of attack— is located near or within a civilian area the one cannot be destroyed without taking the other. This is called double effect and has long been recognized by just war theorists. In the period of knightly chivalry the enemy felt morally bound to keep civilians away from conflicts, and it was easy to avoid double effect. Today it is difficult. To say that no target may be attacked if loss of civilian lives is entailed would permit an enemy to protect every strategic installation by locating civilian hostages near it. To say that there is no difference between soldiers and civilians because both contribute to the war effort is to blind oneself to important distinctions in degree and intention between military forces and those civilians who are found, often by accident, near their base of operations. Although double effect cannot always be avoided, it should never be accepted without rigorous scrutiny of its necessity.

The just conduct of war also involves the fair treatment of military prisoners. They may be confined and disarmed but not tortured, starved, mutilated, or brainwashed. They may be imprisoned and guarded but not morally obligated to give up efforts to escape. They should not be impressed into the service of their captors to aid their war effort or to further their political propaganda. Serious problems arise when one nation agrees to abide by these standards in the treatment of prisoners while an opposing nation ignores or scorns them. But in the final analysis a just war perspective specifies only the conditions to be honored by those professing to accept the teaching and not what can be expected in the practices of others.

The several criteria for determining the justice of any particular war constitute an imposing array of critical insight and analysis. They specifically endorse the use of armed coercion to maintain or to establish conditions of peace and justice while at the same time implying limits upon the legitimate exercise of military force. However, just war teaching has been more impressive on the theoretical level than significant in qualifying or halting particular wars. Even those who agree on principles can argue in particular cases whether all possible solutions short of conflict have been exhausted, whether military operations protect more than they destroy, and whether humane restraints against wanton destruction have been observed. To say, therefore, that a particular war is "just" is to describe the judgments made about it by a particular individual or a particular group and not to report an objective condition concerning which all observers agree. There have only been wars that some men have considered just and wars that some men have considered unjust.

Just war theory arose under the rule of kings and princes. It guided the monarch, and later the magistrate, by specifying the conditions and limits within which each might legitimately resort to the use of arms and the cautions to be observed in guiding their de-

31

ployment. By developing a moral atmosphere prior to the outbreak of hostilities, the just war heritage has affected many conflicts in Western history, helping to determine their character and at times serving to restrain their fury.

The just war theory has also functioned to assure simple citizens that obedience to the ruler is a Christian duty. Augustine admonished individuals to obey even the commands of pagan authorities in the preservation of public order. He declared that a private individual who obeys a king's command to fight is innocent of wrongdoing even if that command is unjust. Francisco de Vitoria, a sixteenth-century Dominican theorist, argued otherwise. He held that if a subject is convinced of the injustice of a war, he ought not to serve in it, even on the command of his prince. Augustine's outlook has generally guided the application of this teaching in Western thinking, but contemporary appeals to just war theory as the ground for individual resistance to national policy may be driving toward Vitoria's view.

Today we are at a critical junction in the use of this concept. If we employ it as a set of considerations for guiding policy debates within democratic societies, we shall be paralleling its main use in the past. Instead of guiding princes and magistrates about when to go to war, it may now help a democracy to debate policy, setting the political tone of a nation. This tone or atmosphere is very important in determining how a nation decides when resort to arms is morally justified. It can also determine whether the nation is willing to observe significant restraints in the conduct of war. On the other hand, if we use the doctrine as guidance for the conscience of the individual in deciding whether or not he should participate in a particular war conducted by his government, we will be enlarging the functional significance of this teaching. Whether the classical theory can bear the weight of this enlarged function is presently a matter of debate.

THE WAR ETHIC OF THE CRUSADE

The classical just war theory occupied Christian attention from the time when Constantine recognized the church to the latter part of the eleventh century. Then the church began to recruit men for a campaign in the East that was designed to free the Holy Land from the rule of Islam. This shifted the grounds upon which participation in war was sanctioned and laid the foundation for a new ethic of conflict. The fundamental premises upon which many people waged war were changed. The crusade, with roots in the Old Testament and in Islam, arrived in Christendom.

a. *The justifying motivations of the crusade tend to be religious and ideological rather than political and practical.* A crusade is fought on behalf of an ideal. It seeks a goal cherished by a particular group. When Christians rushed to free the Holy Land from "infidels" they were motivated by a deep-seated belief in the righteousness of their cause. Pope Urban, in a speech at the Council of Clermont in 1095, admonished his followers to march upon the Muslims with these words: "Hasten to exterminate this vile race from the lands of our brethren, and to bear timely aid to the worshippers of Christ."[5] In the Decretals of Gratian, written about 1150, we find the flat declaration: "The enemies of the Church are to be coerced even by war."[6] In 1917, American Christians entered a struggle in Europe to "make the world safe for democracy."

Whereas the just war arises as a last resort to cure a political wrong or to deal with a matter of injustice that cannot be solved on the level of negotiations, the crusade usually springs from a self-righteous allegiance to an ideal. In religious terms the crusade fights for the holy god of one group by fighting against the devil in an adversary. The righteousness of the cause is unilaterally defined. It is supported by a fervent appeal to devotion. The crusade separates the "good" forces of one side from the "evil" forces of the other and encourages a different measure of fairness in the judgment and treatment of each.

While the just war ethic is always judgmental about what an adversary *does* and seeks to counteract his actions because they threaten justice and order, a crusade ethic easily takes a judgmental stance about who an enemy *is* and seeks to eliminate his very right to exist. In one case, when an enemy has changed his ways he will be allowed to pursue his own destiny. In the other the drive is either to punish or to destroy rather than merely to bring changes in policy and behavior. The conditions presupposed for victory under the first set of premises will be quite different from those under the second set. An enemy will more readily change his behavior than he will surrender his life.

Other religions have taught an ethic of the holy war. In the Shinto religion, participation in war is a means of showing patriotic fervor, of serving the divine emperor. Military life is a channel of religious activity, a ritual marking a cultic group. In Islam, which teaches the value of jihad (or Holy War), Allah is served by an active attempt to crush his enemies. The Muslim teaching of monotheism is often coupled with an admonition to oppose all polytheism and to destroy contenders to Allah. Missionary zeal consists in part of hostility for the infidel. The devout Muslim truly believes that "paradise lies with the sword."

While Christianity has not formally taught a concept of the holy war as a religious duty to be actively sought, it has frequently condoned many of the attitudes associated with the kind of war fought for essentially religious reasons. In the First World War a great majority of religious people in the United States gave an unqualified degree of support to the Allied cause. Ray H. Abrams has documented the story of this support under the arresting title *Preachers Present Arms*.[7] Henry Churchill King, of Oberlin College, declared, "It is neither travesty nor exaggeration to call this war on the part of America a truly Holy War."[8]

b. *In the ethic of the crusade the task of the soldier becomes highly honored and is often believed to bring extrinsic religious rewards.* When the Muslim engaged in the jihad, he did so with an assurance that martyrdom for Allah ensured a certainty of salvation not available to the ordinary faithful. The ordinary Muslim, regardless of his virtue, expected to undergo a final trial judgment reviewing his entire life and determining his claim to an eternal reward. The martyred soldier could count on full and immediate salvation. Participation in war was thus turned into an act with meaning and significance far more momentous for the individual than any political consequences or

35

policy outcome. By taking to the sword the soldier not only sought a practical policy objective, not only defended his homeland or his religion, but also ensured the salvation of his soul.

Christian popes during the Middle Ages followed Muslim teaching, perhaps unwittingly, when they extended blanket indulgence to all who fought in the Crusades. They gave Christians a distinctively positive rationale for becoming soldiers. This was a far cry from Augustine's assertion that participation in war should always be accompanied by a sense of tragedy and involvement in evil! War, rather than a predicament from which even its participants come to realize the frailty of humanity, was made into an instrument for displaying the glory of chivalry and attaining eternal life. The evangelist Billy Sunday, offering the sawdusted version of plenary indulgences during the First World War, declared, "The man who breaks all the rules but at last dies fighting in the trenches is better than you Godforsaken mutts who won't enlist."[9]

Secular idealists of a particular stripe like to suppose that the fury of the Holy War and the self-righteousness of the crusade have been entirely dependent upon a supernaturalistic religion with its appeal to rewards in the afterlife. They have contended that religion breeds war by holding out the promise of special rewards to the soldier. They have even implied that with the demise of supernatural religion military fanaticism will vanish. But the use of military service as a measure of valor does not depend for its perpetuation upon the traditional otherworldly modes of finding extrinsic virtue in military services. Nations have

36

made cultural heroes out of their boys in uniform, granting them an acceptance and reward even in this life. The young man who joins the service and displays his valor obtains public acceptance far beyond what he might be given for ordinary expressions of good citizenship. The respect shown a hero is to a culture of nationalistic concerns what the veneration of the saints is to a culture of supernatural expectations. Depending upon the circumstances, the war ethic of the crusade provides one or both fulfillments.

c. *A crusade ethic erodes those restraints upon military action which are present in just war teaching and even culminates in vindictive hostility toward the enemy.* In a crusade the distinction between believer and infidel, between friend and enemy, between the virtuous and the evil, becomes so sharply drawn that any actions that destroy the enemy are condoned with minimal moral scrutiny. The distinctions observed in just war between combat forces and noncombatants is erased, and double effect is ignored. Many of the most flagrant excesses in war—brutalities in method, barbarism in action, and a lust for total revenge—have stemmed from campaigns undertaken with the self-righteous motivations of the religious crusader.

In a crusade the enemy is hated for who he is, even more than for what he does. It is natural, therefore, to seek his destruction (at least the destruction of his will) rather than his correction. Indeed, it is often hoped that this destruction will entail punitive suffering and be as total and as devastating as possible. This transforms the moral outlook from that in a just war and may even affect the conduct of military operations. One casualty is a sense of proportion in matters of truth. It is easy to propagate hate rumors and to believe the most bizarre reports of enemy malconduct while presuming that friendly troops never ravage land or commit atrocities.

Another casualty in a crusade is the sense of compassion. Crusaders, even those capable of chivalry and honor within their own group, often spill blood with seeming delight and appear to rejoice in those victories which visit upon an enemy a measure of agony beyond that necessary for his defeat and capitulation. When Jerusalem was conquered in the Crusades, Raymund of Agiles remarked, "It was a just and splendid judgment of God, that this place should be filled with the blood of the unbelievers, when it had suffered so long from their blasphemies." During the First World War, clergymen in one American city exercised their imaginations devising cruel and unusual punishments for the Kaiser. According to the account:

> Some said, "Hang him by the thumbs and let him starve"; others said, "Bury him up to his neck and then place food and water in front of him and let him die with food and water in sight"; others, more bloodthirsty, said, "Hang him by his thumbs and cut pieces of flesh out of his body day after day until he was either dead or until there were no more pieces of flesh to cut out." Of all that expressed themselves only one said, "Judge not and ye shall not be judged."[10]

d. *The spirit of a crusade encourages a rhetoric of absolutism which leads to the total psychological mobilization of a nation and threatens to destroy discriminating judgments about both the conduct and the goals of a conflict.* Not only is the crusade character-

38

ized by hatred of the enemy but it sweeps into its vortex every segment of the participating community to produce a total effort for absolute victory.

Distinctions between soldiers and civilians, between combatants and noncombatants, between military and nonmilitary objectives tend to blur in a crusade. Each nation is treated as a whole. The enemy is attacked as a monolithic being and as much damage is visited upon him in as many ways as it can be inflicted. Similarly, as much contribution as possible is extracted from each person at home. No segments of either friend or foe are considered outside the military posture. Defense workers, civil defense volunteers, propagandists, and ordinary citizens share equally in the conflict and are equally expected to be zealous for it.

While this psychological mobilization may occur as an independent development, it may be accompanied by an economic process in which all the resources of the nation are bent to the military venture. A complete mobilization of resources occurs most rapidly in political totalitarianism, but it can take place with alarming rapidity and effectiveness in a democratic society when conditions are right. The freedom of the individual to remove himself from the national effort, to voice effective challenge to its premises, or to disassociate himself from its goals can be severely curtailed. When a nation goes "all out" it sweeps into the service of war every potential economic and human source of support.

A demand for total and absolute victory represents the loss of discrimination regarding the goals of war. One symbol of such a demand, used in the Second

World War, was the slogan "unconditional surrender."
As a means of appealing for completeness of effort at
home, it served a psychological function. It led people
to suppose they were truly engaged in the complete
elimination of evil. Zealots could relish the picture of
an enemy whimpering submissively for mercy as the
price of readmission into the community of nations and
might even do so without thinking of themselves as
engaged in vindictive hatred.

The main result of crusade morality has been to
increase the fury of war in the supposed interests of a
holy cause. In his study of contemporary American
thinking about war, Robert W. Tucker has shown that
as a nation we have basically opposed the use of military methods to achieve national objectives. At the
same time, we have been willing to take up arms to
resist overt aggression, even when that aggression is
aimed against our neighbors and not ourselves. But
paradoxically we have also believed that once force,
which we are reluctant to initiate, is used, our power
should be exercised without restraining limits in order
that an aggressor may be fully punished. Americans
like to win in a big way. Thus, while in one respect our
reluctance to use force except to stop aggression has
borne a resemblance to traditional just war thinking, in
another and perhaps even more decisive respect our
national posture in the conduct of war has expressed a
crusade morality.[11] Robert Osgood has made the same
point as follows:

> If moral sensibilities forbid the use of war as an
> instrument of national policy, they do not prevent
> the use of war as an instrument of ideology, once

war has become unavoidable. In a sense they encourage this; for tender consciences find in broader, more exalted goals a kind of moral compensation for the enormity of war and a rational justification for their contamination with evil. Thus the very ideals that proscribe war become the incentive for fighting war. An aversion to violence is transmuted into the exaltation of violence.[12]

AGONIZED PARTICIPATION

The moral response to war for which the term "agonized participation" is descriptively appropriate appeared with greatest clarity during the Second World War and was accompanied by a revival of a theology in which the plight of sinful man was understood with radical seriousness. This outlook broke radically with the self-righteousness of the crusader and returned to the Augustinian realization that in war the plight and predicament of sinful man is seen with special clarity. The influence of this perspective, summarized by the saying that "war is hell, not sin," was widespread in the Second World War and may even have made the spirit that characterized the pursuit of that conflict different from the spirit of the First World War and its greater use of crusade morality.

a. *This position believes that while war can never be an act of justice it may sometimes be necessary for the prevention of a greater evil that would result from permitting morally perverse power to gain political dominance*. Agonized participants are postpacifist. They freely acknowledge that war is a tragic event,

41

that it is based upon actions at variance with the love ethic of the gospel, and that it cannot have significantly positive effects. But they also proclaim that the morally responsible Christian may face circumstances in which he has no choice but to use war in order to maintain the minimal conditions of human decency in the international order. Reinhold Niebuhr put it this way:

> Once it is recognized that the stubbornness of human selfishness makes the achievement of justice in human society no easy matter, it ought to be possible to see that war is but a vivid revelation of certain perennial aspects of human history. Life is never related to life in terms of a perfect and loving conformity of will with will. Where there is sin and selfishness there must also be a struggle for justice; and this justice is always partially an achievement of our love for the other, and partially a result of our yielding to his demands and pressures. The intermediate norm of justice is particularly important in the institutional and collective relationships of mankind. But even in individual and personal relations the ultimate level of sacrificial self-giving is not reached without an intermediate level of justice. On this level the first consideration is not that life should be related to life through the disinterested concern of each for the other, but that life should be prevented from exploiting, enslaving, or taking advantage of other life. Sometimes this struggle takes very tragic forms.[13]

This position admits the inevitability of guilt, which it finds alike in the position of the soldier who fights and the pacifist who chooses not to do so. Both are caught in the tragic ambiguity of historical choice. The question then becomes, Which course involves the lesser evil: severance from the corporate actions that defend civilized order against a threat from tyranny or the use of military action to preserve tolerable conditions of justice and order?

The Christian Century, through the pen of its former editor Charles C. Morrison, argued that once war has begun, the examination of issues must be in terms of national commitments and not moral ideals. The pacifist who judges war to be morally wrong, while probably right in the abstract, ceases to be relevant once the nation is at war. The decision to fight is a tragic necessity, but the refusal to cooperate is but a futile gesture that also involves moral compromise.[14]

The term "nonpacifist," which was used during the Second World War to describe those supporting the war on the grounds of a tortured Christian sensitivity, bears its own subtle witness to the inner logic of this position. "Militarist" does not fit because it implies the acceptance of warfare as a morally virtuous action, as a positive belief in the efficacy of coercion. "Nonpacifist," on the other hand, suggests that while the abstract moral impulse of the gospel is pacific, there are times when it is crucial to resort to arms in the defense of the right to believe that gospel.

Most men, when they go to war, convince themselves that it serves a noble purpose. They either whitewash war or toss out their Christian scruples in order to accept the demands of combat with the least amount of tension. But the agonized participant acknowledges the necessity without obscuring the tragedy. Roger Shinn entered the Second World War with a strong sense of the need to stop Nazi tyranny. Spurning both his ministerial exemption and the noncombatant role of a chaplain, he entered as a private in the infantry. But as he interpreted the war and his actions in it he took pains to show that war is unlovely and to acknowledge how it contradicts the ideals of Christian faith. He admitted that it disrupts normal morality, that it divides the church, and that it strikes at the very roots of faith. Calling his fellow Christians to those actions and attitudes which alone can take a country beyond the mere negations of military victory, he became one of his generation's most thoughtful examples of the agonized participant.[15]

    b. *The agonized participant insists that war must be conducted with contrition and kept free of vindictive hatred for the enemy.* Men who go to war as citizen-soldiers usually believe their cause is just; that of the enemy, evil. They fight believing that the enemy is guilty, unfit to live among the family of nations because he has pursued policies that disregard law and order. Especially in the atmosphere of a crusade the guilt is presumed to lie with the enemy. "Get the infidel," "Destroy the Hun," and "Crush the aggressor" pour forth as rally cries. Agonized participants are more likely to make the following confession: "We know that our enemies were guilty, but we were guilty too. Although we protest that our sins were less than theirs, we know when we look at the Cross of Christ that nothing justifies us. We cannot fight against wrong without confessing that we are guilty of the wrong."[16]

    No group at war likes to pause for this kind of moral self-examination. When sentiments like these crept into the sermons of chaplains in the Armed Forces their commanding officers winced. The call for men on the "right" side to acknowledge guilt was like grit within the ears of those strongly loyal to the nation, responsible for zeal, and devoted to the destruction of an enemy. It seemed like a halfhearted way to do an important and a necessary job.

In the opinion climate of the home front such acknowledgments were equally unpopular. The conscience of the crusader, even among civilians, has never nurtured a well-cultivated sense of moral ambiguity, nor has the psychology of conflict naturally bred a desire to identify oneself, however partially, with the shortcomings of the enemy. Agonized participants who attempt to stem truculent self-righteousness and vindictive hatred during wartime are hardly sliding along a path of least resistance!

c. *Military victory, while necessary, is but a negative attainment that clears the way for subsequent political and social programs designed to reestablish reasonable justice and order.* Instead of showing a "Hit it hard and get it over quickly" attitude during a war, the agonized participant gets in for a long, slow haul of social and political reconstruction following the cessation of hostilities. War is defended as a precondition to solving a political or social problem in the international sphere, not as a solution. To defeat an enemy is not to make a friend, to force a nation to its knees is not to create a partner in the world community.

It takes wisdom, spiritual maturity, and patience to accept the burdens of reconstruction following the cessation of hostilities. The agonized participant does not forget, nor would he let his fellow countrymen for-

45

get, the tasks that follow in the wake of every military success.

The impact of these perspectives, represented in significant proportions within both the statesmanship and the ecclesiastical leadership of the nation during the Second World War, may have been considerable. Many pulpits, while accepting the necessity of war, preached, "Thou shalt not hate, even when fighting." They also called the nation to shoulder its continuing responsibilities as both a sternly benevolent occupying force and a partner in the urgent tasks of reconstruction. It is a record of which this nation may be justly proud despite the disillusionment that has occurred with its failure to secure a completely enduring peace.

d. *Lastly, the agonized participant acknowledges the right and privilege of conscientious objection to war even though he disagrees with those Christians who consider themselves called to this witness.*

All too few just war theorists, despite the possibility that their teaching may yet acquire significance for moral objection to particular wars, have defended the moral legitimacy of conscientious objection to all wars or worked to extend and protect the freedoms of individuals called to take such a stand.

Agonized participants break with this perspective, as they also do with the hatred and contempt sometimes shown to conscientious objectors by a general public in wartime. While they deny through a vigorous polemic the claim of some pacifists to have a more advantageous and strategic way to deal with armed tyranny, they never accuse the pacifists of bad faith or moral turpitude. The agonized participant may criticize as politically naïve the perfectionism he sees at

46

the heart of the pacifist position, but he respects and accepts conscientious objection as a valid witness to a truth in the gospel. Conscientious participants have sought and defended the fair treatment of conscientious objectors and sought to maintain fellowship with them in the life of the church. Rather than resenting the pacifist as a coward or a traitor, the agonized conscientious participant has welcomed his witness even while denying as vigorously as possible the pragmatic preference of pacifism to the agonized use of armed resistance against tyranny and injustice.

III. RELIGIOUS OPPOSITION TO PARTICIPATION IN WAR

Opposition to war and violence on religious grounds is ancient in heritage and widespread in appearance. In China, six centuries before the birth of Christ, the sage Lao-tzu wrote: "He who with Reason assists the master of mankind will not with arms strengthen the empire," while in India, Gautama Buddha declared: "No one should attack a Brāhmana, but no Brāhmana, if attacked, should let himself fly at his aggressor! Woe to him who strikes a Brāhmana, more woe to him who flies at his aggressor."

48

Moreover, religious opposition to war has been enormously potent, inspiring heroic martyrdoms, mass protests, and withdrawal from the privileges afforded by coercive society. Men have chosen to die rather than to take up the sword, to rot in dungeons rather than to don the uniform of their country. They have suffered the pangs of social ridicule, the wounds of disinheritance, and the misfortunes of political banishment for the sake of conscientious obedience to a pacifist reading of the love ethic of the gospel. Bold in their steadfast allegiance to conscience they have even suffered an ultimate irony: dismissal as "cowards" by unsympathetic compatriots!

Opposition to war on religious grounds can be found in every age of Christendom, though some periods have seen more of it than have others. A generation raised upon a cold war psychology cannot remember, for example, when at least three of the most significant pulpits in New York City were occupied by men who had admitted and vocal pacifist convictions. One of these, having participated in the First World War, preached a resounding sermon in The Riverside Church in 1934 addressed to the Unknown Soldier. The sermon, which was inserted by a sympathetic congressman into the *Congressional Record,* ended with this resolution.

At any rate, I will myself do the best I can to settle my account with the Unknown Soldier. I renounce war. I renounce war because of what it does to our own men. I have watched them coming gassed from the front line trenches. I have seen the long, long hospital trains filled with their mutilated bodies. I have heard the cries of the crazed and the prayers of those who wanted to die and could not, and I remember the maimed and ruined men for whom the war is not yet over. I renounce war because of what it compels us to do to our enemies, bombing their mothers in villages, starving their children by blockades, laughing over our coffee cups about every damnable thing we have been able to do to them. I renounce war for its consequences, for the lies it lives on and propagates, for the undying hatreds it arouses, for the dictatorships it puts in the place of democracy, for the starvation that stalks after it. I renounce war and never again, directly or indirectly, will I sanction or support another! O Unknown Soldier, in penitent reparation I make you that pledge.[1]

Thirty-three years and several conflicts later a Negro leader who had captured the imagination of his people and the admiration of the world in a nonviolent struggle for racial justice mounted the same high distinguished pulpit and flatly condemned American involvement in another war. He saw the war as destroying not only the bodies of enemies and combatants but the soul of our nation. "If America's soul becomes totally poisoned," he observed, "part of the autopsy must read Vietnam. It can never be saved so long as it destroys the deepest hopes of men the world over."[2]

In speaking about opposition to war we do not mean an aesthetic dislike of conflict—shared even by many zealous military men. Any opposition based only upon dislike of war's procedures, resentment of its privations, or discontent with the disruptions of normalcy that follow in its wake deserves no serious respect. The slacker does not oppose war; he dodges it. War is not wrong because it involves high risks to our lives and limbs, but because it forces men to hunt out and destroy other men. Willingness to sacrifice convenience, freedom, and even life itself may be involved

50

in opposing war. War is rejected morally and conscientiously only when its methods or purposes arc held to be fundamentally wrong.

Opposition to war all but demands a religious foundation, though not necessarily a theistic belief, for its sustenance. Humanists and anarchists who oppose war on general or philosophical grounds may still be said to express a religious conviction despite the fact they are not supernaturalists and may not participate formally in the life of a worshiping community. Men are unlikely to maintain the steadfast and perhaps even dogged devotion to an ideal demanded of the conscientious objector unless their conviction is rooted in a pervasive and overwhelming concern.

Pragmatic politics seldom furnishes a sustaining foundation for opposition to war. Statesmen may plea for peace or seek disarmament if either advances the national interest. They can even put up the sword when it is situationally expedient to do so as part of statecraft. But they cannot witness profoundly against war itself. Likewise, in general, the business sense perceives too much at stake in terms of public relations and financial involvement to become a decisive source of opposition to war. In many cases the same is true of the educational enterprise, which is either a tool of the state or dependent upon the establishment.

Despite rootage in a fundamentally religious conviction, pacifism is not of one piece. Think of the diverse backgrounds from which pacifists come! One may be raised in the isolation of a Mennonite countryside, separated from the main currents of contemporary life. He may have ended his education at eighth grade in a parochial school taught by members of his own tradition. Another may come from a suburban family, a product of affluence. He may have traveled through several foreign lands and have graduated from a highly competitive college. His church membership may be with a congregation in which the majority of members are hardly aware of his position and probably hostile to it. Still a third pacifist may live with social activists dedicated to the transformation of society or among a peer group largely interested in disassociating itself from the mainstream of society.

In speaking of pacifism, therefore, it is important to think of variations on a theme. The variations are crucially important for analysis and understanding. Whereas all pacifists reject war in some way and at some point, they differ in their motivations, their reasons for taking such a stand, and even their intentions and goals. There are pacifists who withdraw from life in a sinful world in order to remain faithful to a moral ideal, but there are also pacifists who would remake the world into a new order based on principles consistent with love and brotherhood. There are pacifists who accept the legitimacy of economic competition— even class strife—but others who regard a competitive economic order as wrong. Some pacifists are political anarchists who see no valid role for the organized structures of society, while other pacifists are ready to accept the rule of princes or magistrates as long as they are not required to sustain that rule by service in an armed militia.

Most Christian pacifism can be understood more clearly if scrutinized in terms of two motifs. In one motif, loyalty to the ideals of peace and brotherhood, usually coupled with obedience to a leader who exem-

52

plifies the way of nonviolence, is uppermost. Pacifism in this motif does not seek to alter, change, or overthrow the social order to which it is related. In another motif, the urge to abolish war becomes a social passion. Pacifists drawn to this outlook seek the transformation of society by the direct and indirect application of nonviolence as an instrument of change. A third type of pacifism—more prevalent perhaps in some Asian religions and their offshoots than in the Christian West —minimizes the distinction between good and evil and thus eliminates the urge to defend one and to overcome the other. While not mutually exclusive, these categories are helpful for analyzing the spectrum of living advocacy that manifests itself as pacifism.

Vocational Pacifism

a. *Vocational pacifism is grounded in obedience to the teaching of a leader or acceptance of the principles of a community that is opposed to participation in war. This obedience is decisive apart from considerations of practical and social consequences.* While vocational pacifists may believe and teach that pacifism is a more excellent way or a more promising strategy for the achievement of human goals than the continued pursuit of conflict, they espouse the pacifist position because of its inherent moral appeal and not because of its promise as a strategy.

The early church was basically pacifist, probably in these terms. Few of its members were soldiers before conversion, and none took up the military life anew once they professed Christ. Many scholars have debated the meaning of the early church's pacifism.

53

Some have suggested that the first-century Christians were mostly concerned to avoid idolatry, such as wearing the heathen costume required of soldiers or rendering obedience to heathen leaders. Bethune Baker, Ernst Troeltsch, and Paul Ramsey have used this interpretation to conclude that a modern pacifist refusal to bear arms cannot be justified by citing as an example the early Christian refusal to participate in the military profession. On the other hand, C. J. Cadoux and Peter Mayer have challenged this argument as an escape from the obvious implications of New Testament teaching and early Christian adherence to it.

Perhaps both considerations were present in the minds of early Christians. They seem to be interwoven with each other in Tertullian's extended discussion of the plight and promise of a young Christian who was martyred for refusal to wear the laurel crown. Tertullian considers whether or not the military service in which the young Christian was engaged was of itself as much a violation of the gospel as would have been the wearing of a pagan symbol.

To begin with the real ground of the military crown, I think we must first inquire whether warfare is proper at all for Christians. What sense is there in discussing the merely accidental, when that on which it rests is to be condemned? Do we believe it lawful for a human oath to be superadded to one divine, for a man to come under promise to another master after Christ, and to adjure father, mother, and all nearest kinsfolk, whom even the law has commanded us to honour and love next to God Himself, to whom the gospel, too, holding them only of less account than Christ, has in like manner rendered honour? Shall it be held lawful to make an occupation of the sword, when the Lord proclaims that he who uses the sword shall perish by the sword? And shall the son of peace take part in the battle when it does not become him even to sue at law?[3]

In dealing with this problem, Tertullian concentrated upon those aspects of military service which involve the compromise of allegiance to God. He counseled new converts from ever taking up military service but specifically noted that the Christian tradition has willingly accepted converts from the ranks of the military without requiring them to change vocations. Tertullian also declared that military service does not provide escape from the punishment of sins, nor exemption from martyrdom.

Much that Tertullian said can be used to bolster a pacifist reading of early church life, but on the main issue as to whether Christians can ever be soldiers his treatise is not clear. There is less uncertainty in *The Apostolic Tradition of Hippolytus*. Listing trades and professions in which Christians cannot engage, it declares:

A soldier of the civil authority must be taught not to kill men and to refuse to do so if he is commanded, and to refuse to take an oath; if he is unwilling to comply, he must be rejected [for membership in the church]. A military commander or civic magistrate that wears the purple must resign or be rejected. If a catechumen or a believer seeks to become a soldier, they must be rejected, for they have despised God.[4]

Vocational pacifism does not rest its case completely upon the call to avoid idolatory. It also entails a refusal to make political effectiveness an overriding consideration in the taking of moral stands. A Reformed pastor in France, writing during the Second World War, put it this way: "If we were studying problems of sexual morality or financial honesty, and tried to resolve them from the standpoint of effectiveness before thinking about being faithful to God, the results would plainly be disastrous. Why should things be any different with the problem of war?"[5]

Christian vocational pacifism takes the New Testament (or the life example of Christ) as the source of its moral guidance. Those sectarian movements of the Protestant left wing which made a moral law book of the New Testament and read its literal injunctions seriously, concluded that Christians should not bear arms. Like the early church these groups banned from membership those who would not abandon the sword and who refused to take an oath. The direct inward certainty of men with conviction on this point is reflected in the autobiography of an early American merchant who decided not to keep arms for protection against robbers.

> When I laid aside my pistols, exchanging them for the protection of the Lord God of Hosts, I was no more tormented with the fear of robbers. . . . I had no more doubt, from the spirit and example of Christ and the precepts of the Gospel, that all kinds of carnal warfare were unlawful for the followers of Christ, than I had of my own existence. At this solemn moment the Word of God appeared a reality; a sure foundation on which to rest my eternal hopes.[6]

Few pacifists are sufficiently naïve to base a whole moral commitment upon a single text or saying of Jesus, but appeals to Scriptural texts have often been made. In dormitory bull sessions, in sermons, in tracts, and even in serious books enormous emotional and sometimes scholarly energy has been expended in citing particular New Testament texts as injunctions for or against participation in war. It is understandable why such "proof text" methods are termed legalistic, but the phrase must be applied with equal candor to both pacifists and nonpacifists who engage in this practice. Biblical literalists often appeal to Biblical texts to justify military service. There is hardly a pacifist alive who has not been challenged with the quotation from Mark 12:17: "Render to Caesar the things that are Caesar's, and to God the things that are God's." It is one of the ironies of history that a phrase which Jesus may have used primarily to avoid a trap has been employed by many of his followers as though it is an evident moral injunction to serve the state by using arms. So prevalent has been the citation of Scriptural passages in defense of participation in war that G. H. C. MacGregor, in one of the most widely used pacifist tracts written in modern times, devoted several pages to refuting proof-text ways of sanctioning war.[7]

The New Testament basis for pacifism does not depend upon hairsplitting over the meaning of single texts. It depends, rather, upon a broadly based realization that the love ethic of the gospel, reflecting as it does the life, teachings, and example of Christ, implies a clear prohibition of killing in warfare. But even those who take the Christian imperative in these terms see different implications in it. Some, such as the Seventh-Day Adventists, believe that only military combatancy is prohibited and willingly enter military service as members of unarmed medical units. Others believe that any cooperation with the instrumentalities of a war effort is wrong and will go to prison rather than cooperate even to the extent of registering for the draft. Some feel that the New Testament condemns the use of violent coercion as wrong but leaves Christians under an obligation to resist evil by other means. Others feel that the New Testament ethic is an ethic of nonresistance to evil—a conclusion with very different moral consequences.

b. *Vocational pacifism expresses a total commitment to a moral ideal that presumes the individual will judge all his actions, and not merely the question of participation in war, by the standards of a love ethic.* This requires more than an intention to be consistent. It presupposes a thrust toward an increasingly perfected obedience to the gospel as a moral response to divine grace.

Many pacifists, largely to the extent to which they show a vocational motif, have accepted the doctrine of perfection as a meaningful way of pointing to the unconditional aspect of love's demands. A. J. Muste argued that we cannot dispense with the doctrine of perfection without destroying something valuable in all of life. The idea of perfection stands, never as the symbol of what has been attained, but as the means of underscoring the totality and all-pervasive character of love. Muste observed that science, art, and human relationships are all dependent upon the thrust toward perfection. No scientist would tell himself, "Well, I am a poor fallible creature anyway, bound to deceive myself," and then proceed to accept a sloppy experimental solution to a problem in order to meet some immediate need.

58

A civilization that has blurred the ideas of obligation to the highest moral standards and accountability to God has no bond to hold it together. A generation that believes itself condemned to moral impotence is doomed to moral impotence and to disintegration.

So it is, finally, in the deepest and innermost realm of all, that of religious experience, that the soul of man thirsts for God, not for a lesser being, and will not rest until it finds its rest in him.

. . . There would be no human life if this binding element of the thirst for perfection and its satisfaction were not in it.

There is, of course, a better keyword to use here than the term "perfection." The keyword is "commitment" or "surrender." It is the purity of heart, the integrity, of which Jesus spoke. It is Kierkegaard's concept, "Purity of heart is to will one thing."[8]

The perfectionistic impulse shifts men's allegiance from a horizontal set of considerations to a vertical ultimacy in which the demands of God rather than the necessities of social order are given priority. This does not mean, of course, that the vocational pacifist is unwilling to be a member of society in those respects in which he can accept such involvement without contradicting his allegiance to God. But he moves toward the full service of the divine rather than complete identification with the needs of the social order. While he never dares to claim that at any time or in any manner he attains perfection—every actual moment is short of the vision—he does not truncate his effort with a theory of ambiguous action tailored to fit the needs of a sin-filled world. He does not ponder the best sin to commit —the lesser evil—and commit it. Or, if he does, it is always that action for which he believes that God rather than human society seems to call.

The thrust toward moral perfection can also serve in vocational pacifism as grounds for accepting nonresistance to evil as the keystone of New Testament teaching. The vocational pacifist, deriving his criteria and the impulse for action directly from God, trusts God's providence to care for history. If God does not choose to eradicate particular political corruptions or social malfeasance from a given situation, the vocational pacifist does not feel that history will be lost. Criticizing a pacifism of nonviolent resistance to evil as unbiblical, Guy Franklin Hershberger declared:

> New Testament nonresistance is concerned first with obedience to God and the creation of loving brotherhood. Desired advantage and social change are secondary to this, and are striven for only in so far as the methods used are not in conflict with the will of God. Nonresistance does not adopt suffering as a means of achieving justice, although it does stand ready to suffer even injustice for the sake of obedience to God, if there is no other way.[9]

The perfectionist impulse often drives men to dramatic forms of total commitment. Albert Schweitzer gave up a brilliant career in theology and music to practice medicine in Lambaréné Africa. Schweitzer's pacifism was based upon the principle of reverence for life and was a clue to his whole life orientation. From the perspective of this principle he diagnosed Western culture as sick and called for a new and totally different response to life. Schweitzer stressed the perfectionist (or absolutist) element in ethics because he believed a worldly relativism cannot get beyond the mere social law to any possibility of saving achievement.

Perfectionism may be accompanied by separatism.

Concern for complete and perfect obedience in one's own life may not be combined with the search for an ethic acceptable to all the world. The Anabaptists totally and completely rejected the use of armed coercion by members of their own fellowship, yet referred to the sword as "ordained for use outside the perfection of Christ." They did not try to construct a Christian ethic acceptable to, and valid within, a community outside of Christian commitment. Their key ethical concept has been total fidelity within the fold rather than universal responsibility within the world, and they have been willing to live apart from the mainstream of the world's life in order to "obey God rather than man."

Religious perfectionism should not be equated with radical absolutism. One seeks totality in obedience to a love ethic of the gospel in devotion to God's will; the other is concerned to be as totally effective as possible in the effort to resist war. The first disassociates itself from war and the social processes that support it as a form of witness to a higher morality; the other protests against war and uses social forces to seek its elimination. When faced with the coercive power of the state, perfectionism generally prompts submission; absolutism, anarchy. The perfectionist believes compromise is morally abortive; the absolutist believes it is strategically defeating.

c. *Vocational pacifism in general does not obstruct the war efforts of conscientious participants.* While no convinced pacifist concedes that the nonpacifist is morally right, the vocational pacifist often respects the legitimate convictions of those who do not agree with his conclusions. In removing himself from war by some degree of restraint he withdraws from, rather than resists, the efforts of the civil order and the participation of his fellow Christians in supportive roles within it. A few vocational pacifists even refrain from debate with their fellow Christians who take a different moral stand, but all refrain from direct actions that are designed to embarrass, subvert, or terminate the activities of conscientious participants.

This may be the most decisive of all criteria for distinguishing vocational from activistic pacifism. The vocational pacifist often recognizes and usually concedes moral legitimacy in the decisions of those who engage in war on conscientious grounds. He carefully avoids any deliberate obstruction that would aid and abet his nation's enemies. He searches for means of maintaining fellowship and dialogue across the differences that separate him from Christian brethren of a different point of view. He applies the principle of reconciliation to the separations that divide the body of Christ on issues of war as well as to the nations that are divided on issues of policy. The vocational pacifist is prepared to trust in persuasion, even in the process of opposing war itself.

Activistic Pacifism

In 1929, Devere Allen made a contrast between "traditional" pacifism, marked by religious devotion to the ideals of a hateless life, and "modern" pacifism. Whereas "traditional" pacifism, as kept alive by the historic peace churches, is marked by renunciation, according to Allen, the pacifism of today is strongly positive. The pacifist's concern is not merely the salvation of his soul by refusal to sin through the employment of violence; he is out to abolish war and conceives of his pacifism as a means directly to that end. The old individualistic type of pacifism, offering the world a "testimony" by example, is of course alive to-day, though the vocabulary is somewhat changed. However, the pacifist who uses his influence as he may in nonconscript countries, and the war resister in more militaristic lands who goes to jail refusing military service, are alike in visualizing a world order ultimately freed from the clutch of the war monster. Regardless of how often pacifists may appear to the public eye as obstructionists, recalcitrants, or slackers, they are undertaking positive accomplishment in social progress.[10]

"Activistic" is a better adjective than "modern" for the kind of pacifism Allen has described.

a. *Activistic pacifism is grounded in a belief that the renunciation of violence is socially imperative and politically effective.* It is concerned to be a part of the ongoing society of men and to influence human affairs through witness and pressure. It believes that society is capable of being transformed from its present coercive ways to a cooperative order. It looks upon the state, not as a device for restraining sin (which by its very nature must be coercive), but as a community of men willingly joined in common endeavors. Hence, the state can be Christianized in its life and character even as individuals can be Christianized. Such pacifism looks forward to the day when "the kingdoms of this world are become the kingdoms of our Lord, and of his Christ."

Quakers have generally advocated a pacifism of the activistic type. Whereas the Mennonites have believed that coercive society is essentially sinful and must therefore be shunned, the Quakers have held that any coercive society is historically abortive and must therefore be transformed. By accepting political office, by engaging in social action, and by bringing the standards of Christian morality to bear upon the corporate life of man, the Quakers have hoped to change society into a more peaceful order—even to achieve a world in which force is not used.

Others have shared this hope. William Ellery Channing did so as a Unitarian preacher. He delivered a discourse on war in the year 1816 before the assembled Congregational ministers of Massachusetts and a second discourse in 1835. In these discourses he argued that war is a passing historical evil and predicted the progressive elimination of coercive violence from the social order. He prescribed for the changes in attitude and outlook required to hasten the desired day. In the first discourse he condemned war for its influences upon the men and nations who conduct it, believing it to unleash throughout the warring community "unfriendly and malignant passions." War springs from human passion for superiority, from false patriotism, and from the appeal of the splendid trappings and ornaments which the young see adorning the soldier. Channing was particularly scornful of the glare of glory that surrounds the military profession.

Channing's confidence that war will eventually be eliminated appears with unmistakable clarity in his last public words.

Mighty powers are at work in the world. Who can stay them? God's word has gone forth, and "it cannot return to him void." A new comprehension of the Christian spirit, a new reverence for humanity, a new feeling of brotherhood, and of all men's relation to the common Father—this is among the signs of our times. We see it; do we not feel it? Before this all oppressions are to fall. Society, silently pervaded by this, is to change its aspect of universal warfare for peace. The power of selfishness, all-grasping and seemingly invincible, is to yield to this diviner energy. The song of angels, "On earth peace," will not always sound as fiction. O come, thou kingdom of heaven, for which we daily pray! Come, Friend and Saviour of the race, who didst shed thy blood on the cross to reconcile man to man, and earth to heaven! Come, ye predicted ages of righteousness and love, for which the faithful have so long yearned! Come, Father Almighty, and crown with thine omnipotence the humble strivings of thy children to subvert oppression and wrong, to spread light and freedom, peace and joy, the truth and spirit of thy Son, through the whole earth![11]

The Social Gospel, which heavily influenced American Protestantism between the two world wars, was also optimistic about the elimination of coercion from society. Many of its adherents were pacifists and all its spokesmen felt the need for Christians to work for the abolition of war. Walter Rauschenbusch, who was perhaps the best-known theologian of the Social Gospel, was more preoccupied with overcoming economic injustices than with the elimination of coercion from society. But, while he was not a complete pacifist, he did find in the struggle against economic injustice places at which he also needed to criticize and to challenge the war system. In believing that the social order could be Christianized he also contributed to the climate of hope in which the Christianization of the international order by overcoming war was viewed by great numbers of Christians as a worthy outlet for their social idealism. George D. Herron, a perhaps less illustrious exponent of the Social Gospel, actually looked for the development of a noncoercive state that would replace a church beholden to the coercive practices of society.

These hopes were reinforced by confidence in man's ability to improve society. The New Testament idea of the Kingdom of God was equated with a better society. Belief in progress seemed self-evident in a culture born of the Enlightenment and nurtured on social Darwinism. Even the First World War was, for a time at least, believed to have made a world secure for peace. Many countries signed instruments such as the Kellogg-Briand Pact outlawing war.

In such a climate of opinion it was comparatively easy to think of the renunciation of coercive violence as a historical possibility. Pacifists continued to hope for a world of peace and justice even when they experienced profound disillusionment with the failure of the First World War to bear the fruits of enduring peace. They rejected the method used rather than doubting the outcome expected. They urged individuals to refuse to cooperate with the evil of war as a means of hastening a period in which war would be rejected as an instrument of national policy. The "peace movement" was to become a crusade against war.

b. *Activistic pacifism specifically advocates the use of nonviolence as a positive weapon for the achieve-*

66

ment of social change. In advocating nonviolence as a morally legitimate form of resistance to evil, the activistic pacifist assumes a very different posture toward the world than does the vocational pacifist. Believers in nonviolence regard the duty to oppose evil by every means short of violence to be an important part of Christian obligation. Martin Luther King became a pacifist only after he realized that nonviolence provides a way in which to oppose evil without the use of military techniques.

The use of the terms "nonresistance" and "nonviolence" in pacifist writing suffers from great confusion. The clarity with which Guy F. Hershberger could draw a distinction between these two terms has been all but lost in subsequent discussions. It was probably obscure even in the writings of pacifists before Hershberger's time. Take, for example, Adin Ballou's description in 1846 of his convictions as a member of the New England Non-Resistance Society.

> It is not non-resistance to animals and inanimate things, nor to satan, but only to human beings. Nor is it *moral* non-resistance to human beings, but chiefly physical. Nor is it physical non-resistance to all human beings, under all circumstances, but only so far as to abstain totally from the infliction of personal injury, as a means of resistance. It is simply nonresistance of injury with injury—evil with evil.[12]

William Lloyd Garrison had the same moral stance in mind when he hailed the Principles of the New England Society to be potentially as important for mankind as was the signing of the Declaration of Independence. He was not thinking, however, of meek sub-

67

mission to the forces of evil when he resolved for the Society "to speak and act boldly in the cause of God; to assail iniquity in high places, and in low places; to apply our principles to all existing civil, political, legal, and ecclesiastical institutions."[13]

Behind the confusion of words that obscures the differences between nonresistance and nonviolence stands a very basic difference between two points of view. In one, advocated by men like Guy F. Hershberger, the touchstone of Christian obligation is nonresistance to evil. In the other, nonviolence is taken as a crucial method for combating evil. Thomas Merton, writing a preface to P. R. Régamey's book *Non-violence and the Christian Conscience*, emphasizes that "not only does non-violence resist evil but, if it is properly practised, it resists evil more effectively than violence ever could."[14]

Richard B. Gregg, in a highly influential book that has done much to present nonviolence as an effective strategy for repelling evil, used terms such as "Moral Jiu-Jitsu" to describe its logic and consequences and drew analogies between the methods and aims of nonviolence and those of violence. The courage, energy, discipline, endurance, and other traits of toughness required of the military soldier can be found in the practitioner of nonviolence. Nonviolence is, as Gregg presented it, a substitute manner for conducting the struggle against evil, differing only in one psychological respect from war.

> The object [of nonviolent resistance] is not to make the opponent believe that he is crushed and beaten and humiliated, but to persuade him to realize that

he can attain security, or whatever else his ultimate desire may be by easier and surer means than he saw formerly. The effort is furthermore to help him work out such new means, not rigidly or on any a priori plan, but flexibly in accordance with the deepest growing truth of the entire situation in all its bearings. The opponent's courage is not destroyed, but merely his belief that his will and desire must be satisfied only in *his* way.[15]

Nonresistance, nonviolence, nonparticipation, and noncooperation—the terms are many by which men have pointed to a moral rejection of armed coercion. Nor does the idea for which such terms are used stem merely from Christian impulses. The Hindu concept of ahimsa, which initially meant "nonharm" or "inoffensiveness," was broadened by Mahatma Gandhi to an ideal similar to love and was reinterpreted to mean nonviolent opposition to evil through civil disobedience and the operation of satyagraha (soul force).

By taking nonviolence as a strategy for overcoming evil, the activistic pacifist feels able to refute the charge that those who oppose the use of violence have no program for fighting injustice. He believes that he has a superior method, a more excellent way of overcoming evil. Not only does he believe that nonviolence is more compatible than violence with the ideal of love central in Christian teaching, but he believes that Gandhi has shown that nonviolent resistance to evil is more strategically successful than armed coercion.

c. *Resistance to war and the war system prompts the activistic pacifist to deny by implication the possibility of a pluralistic Christian witness on the legiti-*

69

macy of war. The activistic pacifist resists war openly, even to the point of thwarting the military operations of his own nation. He may picket recruiting centers, lie down in front of troop trains, refuse to cooperate with draft machinery.

Radical expressions of activistic pacifism are not condoned by all pacifists. Vera Brittain once remarked that the actions of "belligerent" pacifists are "nothing other than a form of inverted militarism."[16] Henry David Thoreau seems only to have supported civil disobedience as a form of disassociation from evil. "It is not a man's duty," he wrote, "as a matter of course, to devote himself to the eradication of any, even the most enormous wrong; he may still properly have other concerns to engage him; but it is his duty, at least, to wash his hands of it."[17] "If the injustice is part of the necessary friction of the machine of government, let it go, let it go: perchance it will wear smooth . . . but if it is of such a nature that it requires you to be the agent of injustice to another, then, I say, break the law."[18]

But the activistic pacifist deems it hypocritical to believe that war is wrong yet allow others to perpetuate it. Unlike vocational pacifists, who can respect the moral legitimacy of conscientious participation in war, the activistic pacifist feels that those who embrace war must be resisted. In speaking of fellow countrymen in the service, one opponent of the Vietnam war cried out, "Murderers have no rights." Who has not met pacifists who, while professing love of enemies as a moral obligation of the gospel, are not long on charity toward the Pentagon? The activistic pacifist can become a crusader in reverse.

TRANSMORAL PACIFISM

A third motif within pacifism stems from entirely different assumptions about the nature of man and history. Unlike the main attitudes prevalent in the Hebrew-Christian West, which traditionally cares about moral values in historical and social conditions, this motif is related to an Eastern nondualism in which the urge to support what is right and to resist what is wrong is overcome by what amounts to a denial of the distinctions by which right and wrong are separated.

Part of a world view radically at odds with the main features of the Biblical tradition, this outlook dissolves the contrast between the good and the bad by merging both into an undifferentiated whole. It undercuts the impulse to defend the right and to struggle against the wrong by declaring that there is no ultimate difference between them. Conflict is eliminated by presuming a unity that overcomes antipathy. Even nonresistance to evil is meaningless if evil is defined away.

To appreciate this point of view requires the deliberate reversal of assumptions that are common to all Westerners. Alan Watts, calling his readers to such a reversal, charges that

> the Hebrew-Christian universe is one in which moral urgency, the anxiety to be right, embraces and penetrates everything. God, the Absolute itself, is good as against bad, and thus to be immoral or in the wrong is to feel oneself an outcast not merely from human society but also from existence itself, from the root and ground of life. To be in the wrong therefore arouses a metaphysical anxiety and sense of guilt —a state of eternal damnation—utterly dispropor-

tionate to the crime. This metaphysical guilt is so insupportable that it must eventually issue in the rejection of God and of his laws—which is just what has happened in the whole movement of modern secularism, materialism, and naturalism. Absolute morality is profoundly destructive of morality, for the sanctions which it invokes against evil are far, far too heavy. One does not cure the headache by cutting off the head.[19]

This transmoral stance begins from such radically different assumptions about human life that it cannot be understood as a moral alternative within the framework of Western thinking. It is an alternative to the entire cultural situation in which war is a problem of conscience for either the pacifist or the nonpacifist. Just as we make no comparison between right and wrong stars when gazing at the heavens after dark, or between right and wrong mountain ranges when looking at beautiful scenery, Watts contends that we must learn to accept historical events without making judgments that lead to anxiety and conflict. Although in very limited areas we may improve and change human life for the better, these areas are subordinate to the overarching unity in the transcendent universe where we must accept things as they are.

Watts has taken some of his ideas from Zen Buddhism. Zen carries this principle of nondiscrimination even to its response to military life. It has often extolled such virtues as chivalry and allegiance to duty. It has even taught the art of jujitsu as a means of throwing an opponent off balance by encouraging him to flay without meeting resistance. This causes him to destroy himself with the momentum of his own arrogant thrusts. In a similar vein the sage Lao-tzu advised his followers not to attempt the remaking of the empire when they became rulers.

> When a minister serves a ruler after the principle of TAO, he will not advise a resort to force of arms to become a great nation. Like returns like. So briars and thorns grow rank where an army camps. Bad years of want and disorder follow a great war.
>
> Therefore, the competent ruler, resolutely restraining his desires, dares not resort to force. Because he is resolute, he will not be boastful, nor haughty, nor arrogant; because he is resolute he will act only under necessity; because he is resolute, he will have no ambition to be powerful.
>
> By the nature of things, when the strength of anything is fully developed, it immediately begins to decay. This means that strength is not in accordance with the principle of TAO. Being not in accordance with TAO, it will soon pass away.[20]

The code of the warrior accepts military style as a social custom without judging it morally as either right or wrong. Like hippies who find enjoyment in wearing old military clothing yet want no part of warfare as a social strategy, the traditional Zen culture accepted military courtesy and chivalry as aesthetically appealing without regarding them as crucial instruments of moral purpose.

A transmoral pacifist would probably be unable to declare himself a conscientious objector to a draft without invoking some principle of moral discrimination alien to his professed world view. Of course, if his perspective on life and society were universalized, there would be neither war nor draft. Thus this view presents us, not so much with a way of dealing with war as a problem of conscience as with an alternative world view that can become significant only if it finds a supporting cultural matrix.

But, dare we dismiss this as entirely irrelevant to Western man? It poses an important issue that cannot be readily ignored. To what extent are we responsible for the morals and conduct of other men or for the conditions of life under which neighbors live? Our involvement as a nation in the turmoil of the present world presumes that we have a duty to arrange and control that world in accordance with our understanding of justice and order. Obviously, if we did not draw sharp and vigorous distinctions between good and evil in the affairs of nations, we would not be involved as we are on a global scale.

In epochs of the past our responsibilities have been limited by lack of communication and slowness of transportation. Isolationism was a geographically given condition not a morally determined position. American Indians had no chance of fighting aggression in Asia. Modern technology has changed this, and in so doing has posed the issue of responsibility to neighbors in a radically wider form. In general, we have taken the plight of others as a matter for our concern and have willingly committed ourselves to defend them—usually, alas, when first convinced that their defense is primarily in our interest.

Jesus once admonished his followers to let the tares grow together with the wheat. He also spoke of a God who permits rain to fall alike on the just and the unjust. These suggestions hint of a transmoral perspective. They also, when translated from their agrarian imagery, raise issues pertinent to policy decisions in an era of global togetherness and highly technicalized war-

74

fare. Shall we incinerate whole areas of a countryside to root out political insurgents?

Perhaps we will answer this with our technology by creating devices that skillfully separate "wheat" and "tares" within nations racked by civil strife. Perhaps we will come to control the "rains" of fortune and circumstance to shape a world in the image of our moral judgments and hence succeed in doing what God has not yet been able to do. If so, we can ignore the issue raised by transmoral pacifism. But if not, we may need to re-examine the working assumptions of policies that take upon themselves the moral burden of the world.

IV. MORALS
AND POLICY

War confronts the corporate Christian conscience with great perplexity. The actions that it demands contradict the spirit of love and reconciliation taught by the gospel, yet the goals for which it may be waged frequently express the very concern for social justice and righteousness that Biblical faith engenders. Its methods flatly contradict much that Jesus Christ seemed to teach about nonresistance and nonviolence, yet the reasons for its use are often based upon a concern to protect a neighboring country from unjust attack or from exploitation by those who dishonor all that Christians believe men deserve as children of a righteous God.

War can both defend and disrupt those structures of law and order which are basic to human civilization. It cannot be embraced without contradicting some fundamental mandates of Christian morality, nor can recourse to it under dire circumstances be refused without seeming to invite social malignancy to overrun the world. Within individuals, war can create both bestiality and moral heroism. It is clear that for now, and for the indefinite future, there are bound to be some Christians who can, and some who cannot, conscientiously participate in armed conflict.

But the moral issues related to participation in war cannot be settled in the abstract alone. Those who find it possible to entertain the moral legitimacy of war are still forced to make judgments about individual conflicts. Just war teaching, for example, demands the examination of both the goals and the methods of each conflict before a military action can be considered either right or wrong. Likewise, agonized participation usually appears as a response to a specific crisis of felt obligation created by an injustice deemed so great as to be intolerable and so entrenched as to require eradication by coercive violence.

This means that the moral question, which asks whether war is right and proper, moves to the policy question, which asks whether war is wise and workable under given circumstances. Men have frequently assumed that the policy question is easier to answer, that once committed morally to using arms in defense of justice men will work together for the cause. This was manifestly the case in the Second World War, when a whole Allied world was agreed on the dangers of fascist totalitarianism. It has been almost as true of our attitude toward Communism during the cold war.

Today, however, we are becoming increasingly aware that men can read circumstances differently even when they agree upon moral principles in the abstract. The debate about Vietnam, which has raged so vigorously in all segments of American society, reveals the difficulties that can arise in weighing the implications of circumstances. This war, which may well be representative of the messy uncertainties and confused alternatives that will mark the conflicts of the future, has polarized opinion as has no previous conflict in this century. Practically every traditional set of moral criteria has been invoked both to support and to condemn it, no less by Christian moralists than by the general public. Even men proceeding from the same assumptions have come to different judgments about it. As judged by any aspiration for consensus, it is a case study in perplexity.

VIETNAM AS A PROBLEM IN JUDGMENT

Some Christians, Paul Ramsey among them, have argued that there are situations when the cause of justice can be served only by unilateral intervention in the affairs of other nations. They see the United States as a powerful nation with corporate responsibilities in a bipolar world. In such a world, marked by protracted conflict, there is no effective international authority sufficiently strong to assume responsibility for main-

78

taining order. Consequently, individual states that possess the means to do so—and this points inevitably to our nation—must assume the tasks and duties of maintaining justice where aggression is threatened. While Ramsey gives just war teaching as the formal rationale for his argument, his rhetoric often sounds like the writing of an agonized participant:

> For us to choose political or military intervention is to use power tragically incommensurate with what should politically be done, while not to intervene means tragically to fail to undertake the performance of responsibilities that are there, and that are not likely to be accomplished by other political actors even when we must judge that there is much political responsibility that simply cannot be assumed by us. Anyone who is impressed only by the immorality and probable ineffectiveness of interventionary action should sensitize his conscience to the immorality and probable ineffectiveness of nonintervention. This is the world which magistrates must somehow govern by particular decrees.[1]

It is well and good to exhort magistrates of just and powerful nations to use power for the protection of weaker nations. But any decision to intervene or not to intervene is a policy decision that depends upon a judgment concerning the seriousness of a given threat. Statesmen must decide when to "jump in" and when to "stay out." Paul Ramsey believes that the guideline for decisions of this sort is a pragmatic calculation. The statesman "will count the cost of one effect upon the other. He will ask how much disorder is worth a calculable preservation or extension of justice."[2]

In the 1940's, Christian realists such as Reinhold

79

Niebuhr fought isolationism within America and urged intervention in Europe to curb the aggressive rise of German power. Their guideline was pragmatic. Thus, in one era and in defense of one policy Reinhold Niebuhr wrote, "Looking at the tragic contemporary scene within this frame of reference, we feel that American Christianity is all too prone to disavow its responsibilities for the preservation of our civilization against the perils of totalitarian aggression."[3] In another era, and about an American policy in Southeast Asia strongly condemned by Niebuhr, Paul Ramsey wrote, "In view of the present state of public opinion in this country, any President of the United States is at least as apt to fail to find a way of using available power in a measure commensurate with what should be politically done as he is apt to use power in excess of the responsibilities that have devolved upon us."[4] How can the polemic of one time become such a source of disagreement in another?

Some feel that we move directly from religious conviction to the duty of intervention. Writing of American presence in Vietnam as a protection of the rights and aspirations of the South Vietnamese, James V. Schall, S.J., has observed:

This is the heart of the matter. For religion does not only teach that we *shall not kill* and nothing else. It also teaches us that we shall be *responsible* for our brother in need, for our brother who is suffering persecution and injustice. We know from experience that these two fundamental obligations can come into conflict. And however free we may be to sacrifice ourselves when we alone are involved, the human race has always judged it to be cowardice when we

> sacrifice someone else because of our unwillingness, whatever the reason, to help when we have the power to do so.[5]

This justifies our presence in Vietnam as an extension of "this nation's historic mission to liberty." Failure to oppose the rise of Communism in Southeast Asia would, it is held, be like the compromise at Munich.

Theologians are not alone in deriving policy from moral imperatives. Secretary of State Rusk, thinking of the Vietnam conflict as resistance to the actions of North Vietnam against South Vietnam, has repeatedly spoken of our duty to "punish" aggression. He believes we must show others who might be tempted to overrun their neighbors that violations of the national sovereignty of smaller countries will not be countenanced by the powerful nations of the Western world.

The choice of the term "punish" is significant. Rusk has not merely said "deter," "turn back," or "stop." "Punish" has ethical overtones and presumes that this nation uses its power for moral objectives. Like "making the world safe for democracy," the phrase "punish aggression" moralizes our actions and justifies what we are doing with a crusade ethic.

Many students of world affairs realize that appeals to moral judgments, like those made by Schall and Rusk, are vulnerable. A war can be either defended or criticized, depending upon which kind of moral teaching is invoked as the basis of judgment. They also note that moral convictions may lead to unfortunate rigidity in the conduct of foreign affairs. In order to avoid the possible futility of moral disagreement and the rigidity of an absolutistic stand, these men turn to political calculations as a touchstone of decision. They believe that a highly pragmatic conception of "national interest" should determine the making of policy, and trust that almost all citizens of a pluralistic society can support a policy that is arrived at in this manner.

Robert A. Gessert, who is interested in Christian ethics personally, but who works in defense analysis, uses this approach to analyze insurgency warfare in general and the policy of American intervention in Vietnam in particular. We are there because of "national interest," which requires us to weigh military factors in relation to political purposes in the light of available resources. While "other considerations" may enter in, including the moral ideals of our heritage and the insights of religious ethics, the primary responsibility of officeholders is to consider the practical factors related to national self-interest. "If ethics is understood to be something other than the search for wise political purposes, militarily prudent operations, and just allocations of resources, then 'ethics' should be treated as largely irrelevant to policy for dealing with any war."[6]

This viewpoint cuts the tension, so evident in agonized participation, between political necessity and moral demand. Politics becomes politics and political decisions become totally pragmatic decisions. The function of religion is to provide men with the stamina, courage, and perspective to accept this manner of decision-making as legitimate and not to impose upon the enterprise any extrinsic tests of right and wrong. In short, there can be neither moral nor theological judgments about war as a problem—only political ones. We might call this "transmoral interventionism."

Manfred Halpern, just as politically concerned

about policy-making as Gessert, finds the subordination of moral factors untenable:

> The technicians of power, having shrewdly rejected the illusion that national and individual morality are automatically the same, stop short and do not see that the unfinished task is to relate national purpose to the kind of international justice that gives security and freedom for justice and love to develop among individuals. Indeed, they tend through the prestigious position of their manipulative power to diminish the citizen's concern with love, till he feels embarrassed by the very mention of it in a context of power. In the insecure world in which we live, national loyalty and solidarity have become more precious to most peoples than justice and love. Still, the existence of a nation, any nation, is not justified except as it and its interventions preserve and enhance the individual's capacity to be wise, just, and to love.[7]

Halpern understands that the abstract moral considerations of theological morality do not dictate policy directly, but he also understands that the contributions from such considerations may be helpful in the formation of policy. Three factors—morality, power, and knowledge—have equal importance. These three factors correspond to what Gessert calls religious ethics, resources, and prudential military consideration. But Halpern does not subordinate the religious/normative element to the other two. He warns just as much against a nihilism that simply manages the tactics of conflict as against a moralism that makes the ethical factor privileged in the triadic relationship between morality, power, and knowledge. Moral considerations must be interwoven into policy considerations but cannot tell us what to do without taking technical factors

83

into account. Intervention should be limited to cases where it is politically viable as well as morally legitimate.

Quentin Quade, a political scientist from Marquette University, agrees with Halpern as to both methodology and conclusions. He feels that decisions balancing the different factors involved in matters of policy must be made by the President in the light of the range of data that he alone possesses. Moral principles taught by church bodies must be borne in mind as he considers the factors involved, but they do not in themselves help to make the specific judgments as to when intervention is politically wise and when it is not. Of the problem of intervention in wars of national liberation he notes, "It is not a separate genus of problem, but simply a species of the traditional problem of the legitimate use of national power."[8] Working with these assumptions, Quade has concluded that our intervention in Vietnam is justified and feasible and serves as a crucial deterrent of Communist expansion. Such expansion will, if not stopped, run the line to other nations as along aligned dominoes.

Just war thinking has been used, as by Father Schall, to favor a policy of intervention. It has also been used to condemn what is being done. Peter J. Riga, of St. Mary's College in California, disturbed by the failure of American Catholic bishops to condemn American policy in Vietnam, addressed to them an open letter that said in part:

How shall we justify the dropping of 680,000 tons of bombs in 1966 alone (one-half the tonnage dropped in Europe for all of World War II) on a small, non-industrialized nation unless we are so naive as to believe that it is being used against some bridges and roads? How shall we justify the spraying of rice crops which make combatant and non-combatant suffer and starve alike? How shall we justify the use of torture by those who are our "allies"? How shall we support a war in which it is conservatively estimated, that, for every soldier killed, there are *at least* ten civilians destroyed? How shall we say that our presence is "reasonable" in a country where whole areas are considered enemy territories and whole villages therein may be bombed or shelled? How shall we support a "presence" which makes of that country a house of prostitution and an economic wasteland for the many poor and destitute? . . .

We are no longer in a "just war" by any traditional standards—no matter what the justice of the war may be; we are in the area of simple barbaric slaughter where ideology and pride will not permit us to move meaningfully toward peace.[9]

Among those who regard national interest as a guide to the making of policy, there are critics as well as defenders of American involvement in Vietnam. Men such as George Kennan and Hans Morgenthau have opposed the very involvement which others, like Gessert, regard as dictated by national interest. One such Christian realist, Samuel H. Magill, stresses the necessity of avoiding moralistic self-righteousness in the formation of policy. He complains of fellow realists that they have developed "a crusading and self-righteous stance toward those parts of the world which are at odds with the United States, whether they are Communist or antagonists within the Western Alliance."[10] Here we discover one Christian realist complaining that other realists are turning into crusaders.

The theoretical frameworks by which men say that they make decisions about these matters do not produce predictable results!

A large group of former agonized participants have strongly condemned our presence in Vietnam. They have come to judge the "lesser evil" to be, not continued conflict and escalation of the war leading to a defeat of Communist insurgency, but de-escalation and eventual withdrawal. John C. Bennett has put this conviction as follows: "We still recognize the necessity for the military ingredient in national power and the moral obligation to use power at times to check power. Yet we believe that the circumstances under which military power is being used in Vietnam are sufficiently different from those under which it was used to defeat Hitler to lead to quite different political and moral judgments concerning the issues raised by this war."[11]

Bennett presents a long and extensive analysis that involves many political judgments. It is misleading to compare the national socialism of one period with the international Communism of the other. The first posed a primarily military threat to stable and established governments; it could be stopped by armed conflict. The second creates political and economic upheaval within countries that have minimal stability; it can be countered only by dynamic alternatives that have greater appeal for men in need. The first was monolithically aggressive; the second has proven to be more open-ended than might at first have been supposed. We even accept coexistence with related political regimes as legitimate policy in many areas of the world. Convinced of the differences between Europe of the 1940's and Asia of the 1960's, Bennett has charged

86

that "those who speak with the most conviction in favor of our Vietnam policy seem to us to be blind to many intangible factors in the Asian situation that could cause military successes to lead to political and moral defeats."[12]

Most of the editorial board of *Christianity and Crisis,* largely composed of men who were agonized participants during the Second World War, signed an editorial on March 7, 1966, breaking with national policy in Vietnam and asserting that we are there "engaged in a war that is destructive to the people whom we claim to be helping, to the peace of the world, and to our best interests."[13] The tactics we are forced to employ "alienate and harm the people we purport to save." They have charged that our national prestige is undergoing great harm and that our posture in the world is turning into a socially reactionary opposition against the rising aspirations of oppressed peoples.

It is a new experience for most of us to witness such divisive disagreement about policy matters, even among men who have rather similar moral principles and policy-making assumptions. The debate over American policy in Vietnam shows that political analysis has been no more successful in settling the issues that divide men on questions of war in the modern context than have been the classical and traditional moral arguments about war in the abstract. Perhaps we have arrived, as Robert McAfee Brown, Abraham J. Heschel, and Michael Novak have called it, at "A Crisis of Conscience."[14] If we are increasingly confronted with this profound divergence in our national life, it is likely to revolutionize our assumptions about the role of a citizen in wartime.

POLICY DISAGREEMENT AS A CULTURAL PROBLEM

Citizens of a democracy are generally accustomed to living with divisions of opinion and with arguments between advocates of different policies. We never doubt the patriotism of those who oppose domestic programs such as farm price supports, an antipollution bill, the poverty program, or even a graduated income tax. At times we even overlook the little acts of resistance or defiance which citizens frequently show toward constituted authority. But in war it has usually been different. During the two world wars citizens found it not only difficult but dishonorable to question the national purpose. Regardless of their own contempt for law on little matters, strident citizens have grown irate against those who do not support the national war effort to the last detail. When war has broken out, the usual impulse has been to "rally round the flag, boys."

The customary unity induced by patriotism during wartime has been eroding under the conditions of undeclared conflict seen in Korea and Vietnam. In the Korean conflict a strongly bellicose segment of our society was upset by a failure to pursue a war "to victory." Its discontent smoldered in frustration with a policy it considered unworthy. Nevertheless, it was difficult to do more than complain about half a loaf when advocating a full one.

In the case of Vietnam, opposition has come from those who have regarded the national policy as wrong in kind rather than as inadequate in degree. This disagreement has had to express itself as protest and has become evident in strong vocal polemics, in vigils, in demonstration marches, and even in civil disobedience.

It has shown up within the counsels of government. Congressmen and senators of enormous prestige and of both parties have been articulate critics of administration policy. No call to the flag has been able to overcome differences felt as profoundly as those about Vietnam.

The desire for consensus in periods of national crisis is understandable. Some defenders of current policy sometimes cajole their critics by suggesting that criticism serves the cause of the enemy. Others are less restrained. They equate dissent with subversion and produce news stories such as this:

Washington, May 5—Members of the House Armed Services Committee demanded today that the Justice Department disregard the First Amendment right of free speech and prosecute those who urge young men to defy the draft law.

"Let's forget the First Amendment," Representative F. Edward Hébert, Jr., Democrat of Louisiana, told Assistant Attorney General Fred M. Vinson, Jr., in a loud voice during hearings on the draft.

"I know this [prosecution] would be rescinded by the Supreme Court," he said. "But at least the effort should be made. It would show the American people that the Justice Department and Congress were trying to clean up this rat-infested area."[15]

One politician has even suggested, presumably in seriousness, that we need to declare war on North Vietnam mainly in order to stifle dissent at home. A formal declaration of war changes the legal standing of certain actions. What can be punished as a misdemeanor in peacetime becomes sedition. Acts of defiance in the Armed Forces stemming forth as conscientious refusals to obey orders are punishable in peacetime by imprisonment; in wartime, if sufficiently serious, by death for treason. There are always some men who believe that all a nation needs is the "guts" to rid itself of peaceniks and it will then have unity of purpose, but when such individuals get too numerous and powerful a country is in danger of going totalitarian.

Ironically, efforts to force a consensus by threats and intimidation may be more ominous in a country racked by disagreements than in a land with a clear sense of national purpose. A nation secure in the righteousness of its own cause can tolerate differences with less likelihood of going off balance than one in which disagreement about policy is vigorous and takes illegal forms. War, especially when a matter of divisive debate within a nation, can charge an atmosphere with vindictiveness and produce conditions that, if not counteracted, will prompt men to hold constitutional procedures in contempt.

It is profoundly disturbing to have defiant resistance to a war take such illegal forms as pouring blood on draft files or blocking access to public offices. Individuals who appeal to conscience to justify actions that go beyond noncooperation to overt disruption raise many ethical problems. Can any social order tolerate appeals above its authority as justifications for acts that would disrupt that authority? When does moral duty legitimately stand above the law?

But it is incomparably more disturbing to find officials who wield tremendous authority and influence seeking to counteract dissent by paralegal means. Such uses of official power, however covert, subtle, or condoned by the public, are a greater threat to democratic process than anything that the single individual can

90

do. Officials who claim a higher impulse than the law while possessing the power of a constituted office contradict the very grounds of their authority. Moreover, because they have the power of legal control they can threaten the constituted safeguards of a democracy in an altogether different way than does the private citizen who engages in civil disobedience. Even the vaguest hints of implied coercion, whether from rumors that government grants are not continued for critiques of administration policy,[16] from vague encouragement to draft boards to take political activities and outlooks into account when granting deferments,[17] from "friendly" admonitions to public figures by the FBI,[18] or from policy scrutiny and recording of names and pictures of public demonstrators, can corrode the luster of democratic society and destroy at home the kind of conditions we wish to be established abroad.

The American public is divided. Disagreement is a cultural problem of major proportions and infects every aspect of our corporate life. Howard Schomer has described our condition as follows:

> The American people are morally strained and politically fractured today as at no other moment since the Civil War. They do not know how to make peace in the jungles of Vietnam or advance justice in the city slums here at home. They will not again know a quiet conscience, true political consensus, or even basic national security until they come to terms with the central social fact of our times—the world-wide revolt of the poor in this 20th century. The whole American people need nothing in this world more urgently than a better understanding of the riptides of rival revolutions in which their ship of state is now heaving and rolling.[19]

91

Many thoughtful students of political and social trends believe that our condition as a people can be greatly helped by the development of a profound new vision of social change and the role we should play within it. Manfred Halpern believes that such a vision constitutes the element of knowledge and insight necessary to the making of wise policy and has called for a new awareness of the changes going on in the world. Such a vision "would allow us to understand the fundamental revolutions now in progress in the world, and hence to develop doctrines of intervention relevant to the politics of modernization."[20] Intervention should be limited to cases where it is politically viable as well as morally helpful. Only long-range planning that considers factors above and beyond balances of power can help us to respond intelligently to the social upheavals of these times.

Halpern believes that insights of this sort belong to the realm of social knowledge. He doubts that theological ethics will help in providing a new consensus. Charles West, on the other hand, suggests that we must develop nothing less than a theology of social change that looks beyond the pragmatism of political wisdom, that understands the revolutionary forces at work in our contemporary world, and that avoids self-righteously polarized distinctions between good and evil.[21]

The three statements about the need for a new social vision made by Schomer, Halpern, and West come respectively from a Christian pacifist, a social scientist with theological interests, and a nonpacifist theologian. They bring together a wide range of thought. Is there any chance that a nation might develop a similar agreement if given the leadership? Can

92

we develop a theory of social change that fits with the facts of modern political conditions? Can we maintain a moral critique of the means to be employed in relating to the contemporary world? Can we come to even a modest agreement about the kinds of social change we will judge acceptable and the kinds we must resist? Can we overcome the split between those parts of the world which say, "We are on the side of change, therefore we shall give our support to any means used to attain it," and those which say, "We are opposed to the means by which revolutionary movements seek to accomplish change, therefore we will oppose the change in order to thwart the dangerous means used to further it."

It is not reassuring to realize how the unity of perspective and political consensus that served to make policy simple in the two world wars were produced. It was the sinking of a ship rather than an agreement about insights that precipitated American involvement in the First World War. The argument in the early 1940's between isolationist and interventionist was not settled by political or theological agreement upon values and principles but by the gut reaction of a nation to a sneak attack upon one of its military bases. Our dominant model for the conduct of the cold war, in which we have responded defensively to the threat of an international conspiracy, may have arisen less from a public awareness of the facts of international affairs than from the charismatic power of a leader like Winston Churchill delivering an "Iron Curtain" speech at a propitious time in history.

Once a people has developed the perspective through which it comes to view the events of its own

93

history every episode naturally comes to be taken as a confirmation of the assumptions. This process can persist despite changes in the operative realities, and can be enormously stifling to the development of new insights and liberating vision. Our ideologies last longer than the conditions that give them birth, yet without some ideas to guide our assessment of the problems of society we drift in a sea of confusion. Can we ever respond with creative leadership in the world unless as a nation we have some idea as to how we wish to see the future shaped? Merely to respond defensively to the overt aggressions of those parts of the world we consider hostile is hardly to maintain a moral initiative. Surely we should not wait for an enemy to perpetrate a blatantly hostile action before developing some consensus understanding of the positive obligations which we ought to assume in this hour of history.

But the development of consensus is perhaps of less importance to a democracy than the maintenance and extension of freedom for individuals to be obedient to their highest moral impulses. Only a simplistic version of democracy prompts us to think of counting noses to determine what is right and expecting all citizens to follow the will of the majority. The protection of minority rights and the guarding of the opportunity both to dissent and to withdraw from the dominant policy of the nation have been characteristics of the American heritage. Indeed, our nation has been the envy of the world because it has been a refuge from consensus coercion and has in decades past attracted to its shores men in search of freedom for their consciences.

94

In many past eras this opportunity has been afforded by the vast expanses of a rural agrarian economy lacking tight central jurisdiction. Policy disagreement has been weathered because the structures of control have permitted the deeply convinced and dedicated dissidents to ride out the issue causing turmoil to their conscience. But today the technical processes of communication and of governmental control find increasingly huge numbers of men under increasingly rigid scrutiny of conduct and destiny. Since 1900 public birth records have replaced the family Bible as a source of information concerning the existence of each citizen, the income tax (now enforced by an "all-knowing" computer) keeps tabs on the resources of each individual, and other public agencies have been created that exercise nearly total thoroughness in their scrutiny of individual activity. These combine to force the individual to reckon with the live issues of public policy as they impinge upon his own understanding of moral duty.

Both the political maturity and the social desirability of a culture may be measured in part by the extent to which it can achieve a working harmony yet maintain freedom both for dissent and for the exercise of fidelity to individual conscience. Compulsion may be necessary in maintaining orderly harmony, but the ideal of a democratic society should be to reduce the compulsion to the lowest point compatible with the achievement of national purpose. A democracy should provide each citizen with opportunities to contribute to the social good in ways that do no violence to his individual convictions concerning right and wrong.

95

Since the avenues for service to the nation are subject, as is all life, to increasingly rigid control by technology, it will require a deliberate effort by the nation to widen the margins of freedom for conscience. The need for such broadening is especially acute in a time of great debate about the moral legitimacy of armed conflicts. To maintain such freedom may be even more crucial to the health of our society than finding some consensus about our role in history, and the need for it even stronger when the consensus we might hope to have continues to elude us. There is no more pressing need in the present juncture of our national history than to devise deliberate ways to widen the margins for conscientious disagreement about participation in war further than they have been opened at any previous period in our history.

V. THE STATE, THE CHURCH, AND CONSCIENCE

In the fall of 1940 a small group of students at Union Theological Seminary in New York refused to register under a newly enacted draft law. Eligible for exemption as theological students—or, declining that, as conscientious objectors—they chose to make an open and public stand against a law they considered morally wrong. The student cabinet, responding to the tension produced within the seminary community by this illegal protest, issued a resolution that said in part:

On registration day, some of us will register in support of the Selective Service Act. Some will register, taking their stand within the provisions of the act, as conscientious objectors. Some will present to government officials a statement of their inability conscientiously to register under the act.

We of the student cabinet affirm that, regardless of our disagreements and in some cases of our strong opposition to policies of others, we will hold in respect and reverence those who in sincerity and humility maintain their loyalty to conscience, and will strive through prayer and devotion in the difficult days ahead to maintain in love the community of the Christian faith.[1]

In contrast, during the fall of 1967 a divinity school student from Yale joined several classmates in turning in draft cards to the Department of Justice as a protest against American policy in Southeast Asia. The deferment of the student was canceled and his father announced to the papers that the son was no longer welcome at home. He even expressed a wish for the youth to change his name. The father, a fighter pilot in the Second World War, explained his attitude by remarking, "They're either loyal Americans or they're not."[2]

Conscience in wartime creates problems for the individual, for the voluntary association, and for the state. Each must decide in the face of differences that run to the very deepest level of human commitment how to respond to persistent disagreements. The incidents just cited are both similar and different. In one, fellowship was maintained within a community despite a profound and painful cleavage; in the other, there was a tragic rupture of one of the most basic human relationships. Even if men cannot bring them-

98

selves to agree upon the moral and policy issues regarding war, they can determine whether or not to maintain freedom for diverse decisions and to preserve fellowship with one another in the face of differences.

FREEDOM OF CONSCIENCE AS A LEGAL PRIVILEGE

The clash between the claim of the community and the promptings of individual conscience reaches an apex in the case of disagreement concerning military service. From the perspective of the state it seems that every individual owes a contribution to the common defense. How else can a sovereign political unit maintain the strength to ward off attacks? From the standpoint of the pacifist, however, the demand that he violate his own highest scruples seems ultimately immoral.

Unlike speed limits, regulations of commerce, and even taxes, which make claims upon but limited aspects of a person's behavior and resources (and which can be avoided by making proper readjustments in one's style of life), military service, if entered at all, cannot be given conditionally. It takes away from men the freedom to determine their daily acts by their own moral standards. For this reason it has often been a problem for conscience, especially with the advent of modern, highly efficient, conscription. Many nations have come to realize, sometimes by perceptive wisdom but too often from bitter experience, that provisions must be made for exempting those with sincere scruples against military service if rancor and injustice to sensitive spirits are to be avoided.

As early as the sixteenth century Holland and

New Zealand excused Mennonites from liability under conscription, and France did so in the eighteenth century. Under American law during the First World War, members of historic peace churches could claim exemption. More recently, as in Great Britain during the First World War, and in the United States beginning with the Selective Service Act of 1940, any person opposed to participation in war on the basis of "religious training and belief" has been eligible for alternative types of service.

In some cases the machinery for handling registrants claiming this exemption has been separate from the regular draft system; in other places, related to it. In some cases men have been assigned noncombatant service in the Armed Forces and in other cases civilian service under independent agencies. In some nations these two kinds of service have both been assigned, depending upon the nature of the registrant's objections.

The task of determining sincerity and of assigning conscientious objectors to alternative service is not easy. Their stand is never popular, especially when other men are being forced against their will to enter military service. The devices available for determining who is sincere, especially when one deals with young men who arrive at pacifist convictions within churches that tolerate both the objector and the sincere participant, are often quite difficult to apply. The treatment of a conscientious objector can consume time that is greatly disproportionate to that needed to handle other cases (particularly if draft boards try to cajole and persuade a young man to see "the futility and error" of his ways). When, through a faulty induction or late-blossoming conviction, conscientious objectors end up under military authority, the problems created are enormous.

Provision for conscientious objection to war has evolved in American practice as a matter of legislative discretion, granted at the behest and under conditions specified from time to time by the Congress. We came very close to having the privilege of conscientious objection written as a guarantee in the Bill of Rights. James Madison included a provision guaranteeing the right of conscientious objection within the amendments he proposed for the Constitution in 1787, but his suggestion was defeated by those who believed that such an amendment would deprive Congress of the necessary discretion needed to maintain a militia. Subsequently, often in response to the suffering undergone for the sake of conscience, we have managed to get some legislative provision for the freedoms we nearly obtained as a constitutional right.

In the middle of the 1800's, exemption from military duty could be purchased by members of "peace churches" for the payment of a substitution fee of $300. In 1917 members of such "peace churches" were granted status as conscientious objectors, but had to perform some alternative service. While 56,830 claims were recognized in that period, only 20,873 were inducted into service as physically and otherwise qualified. Noncombatant service was rendered by many men in the quartermaster, engineer, and medical corps. Of those refusing all military service, 3,989 men went to special camps, some 1,500 were furloughed to farm work, and 450 were imprisoned by military courts and sometimes treated harshly by the authorities.

The Selective Service and Training Act of 1940 granted general exemption for two forms of conscientious objection. It provided those who, like Seventh-Day Adventists, oppose only combat status with assured assignment to noncombatant service. This has been defined by presidential authority as service in the medical corps and does not involve training with or use of weapons. For others, the act provided for Civilian Public Service in camps set up by peace churches and supervised by the Selective Service System. The Act of 1940 also made the basis for claims individual conviction rather than identification with a peace church. In specifying who could claim exemption, the law set forth three criteria: (1) religious training and belief; (2) sincerity of conscience; and (3) total pacifist convictions. The provision of the 1940 law has been carried into the 1948 and 1967 reenactments in these terms:

> Nothing contained in this title shall be construed to require any person to be subject to combatant training and service in the armed forces of the United States who, by reason of religious training and belief, is conscientiously opposed to participation in war in any form.

Under the law of 1940 some young men claimed exemption on grounds that did not entail association with religion in the more customary sense of belief in a Supreme Being. The "political" objectors, often troublesome to the draft system in the process of classification and induction, met with less public favor than

102

"religious" objectors. Congress became concerned to avoid exempting those whose motivations stemmed from political conviction and in 1948 included this specific definition of "religious training and belief":

> An individual's belief in a relation to a Supreme Being involving duties superior to those arising from any human relation . . . [which] does not include essentially political, sociological, or philosophical views or a merely personal moral code.

It should have been obvious from the start that this definition of religion would cause trouble. To regard only a belief in a Supreme Being as religious was to exclude many world views that think of themselves as fully convictional in character and hence also entitled to the provisions of the law. As written, the law made special provision for one form of religion to the exclusion of others and hence raised constitutional issues.

In 1965, the famous Seeger case reached the Supreme Court. Daniel A. Seeger claimed exemption as a religious person but refused to affirm his belief in a Supreme Being. The Second Court of Appeals, in ruling on his case, held that the 1948 law violated due process and was unconstitutional by the fifth amendment because it favored one form of religion over another. But the Supreme Court evaded the constitutional question by suggesting the Congress had intended to separate all religious objection in general (including nontheistic types of religious objection) from political, philosophical, and sociological (i.e., nonreligious) objection. Seeger was granted his status as a conscientious objector by a curious casuistry that attributed to Congress understandings at best inferential (and more likely downright contradictory) to the language of the act. The key test became whether the belief in question "occupies in the life of its possessor a place parallel to that filled by the God of those admittedly qualifying for the exemption."[3] While this decision is now mainly of historical interest because the troublesome "Supreme Being" clause was omitted when the act was extended in 1967, the issues it raises may still have to be dealt with in other configurations. The semantic tangles here could become enormous. What would be the status, for example, of a Christian theist determined to base his case upon a "nonreligious" interpretation of a Christianity for a "world come of age"?

While religious training and belief constitute the first test for exemption, two other tests are also imposed. The second is sincerity or honesty of conviction. This is difficult to measure. The burden of proof seems to rest upon the registrant to establish his sincerity. In filing a claim for recognition as a conscientious objector, the registrant is required to submit Form 150, which details his background, religious training and activity, and the basis of his convictions. This form also calls for references who can vouch for sincerity. Two questions on the form are designed to explore into the thinking of the person making the claim. The first of these, "Do you believe in a Supreme Being?" was directly pertinent under the 1948 law but may not be entirely legitimate under the judicial reinterpretations of that law or the revisions subsequently made in it. As part of this question the registrant is asked to explain how his religious belief leads to an opposition to war.

The second question on Form 150, which deals with the central question of theological outlook, asks, "Under what circumstances, if any, do you believe in the use of force?" In practice those who can answer this with a resounding "none" are likely to find their claim most readily sustained. This is because the third test for exemption is opposition to war *in any form*. Those who can honestly affirm a belief that the use of force is never morally justified generally run the best chances of being granted status as sincere objectors.

But the language here is imprecise. A registrant might answer that he believes in the use of force to pry the lid off a can of paint yet be completely opposed to all forms of war. He might even believe in the use of force by civilian police and still be opposed to armed conflict between nations. Draft boards and even scholars who deal with these matters have tended to suppose that opposition to all uses of force is a prerequisite for sincerity as a conscientious objector. They have thus confused the issue. In the court case *Annett v. U.S.* this confusion was clarified. Upholding the right of a person to claim conscientious objection while also admitting the legitimacy of killing in self-defense, the Tenth Circuit Court of Appeals declared, "The mere fact that he was willing to fight in defense of his own life does not mean that he did not have good faith religious scruples based upon the teachings of his church against the command of his country to go to war and kill therein."[4]

While an opposition to the use of all force makes a consistent pacifism, it does not necessarily make a valid test of sincerity. The courts have rightly countermanded the judgments of Selective Service officials

105

who have taken opposition to all use of force to be a prerequisite to classification as a conscientious objector. War is but one form of force, a very violent and ultimate form that raises special moral issues. Ralph Potter has rightly suggested that the only pertinent consideration is the attitude of the objector to *war,* which is but one subspecies of violence.

> The courts have enforced more precise adherence to the words of the statute. The statute itself might have been more precise. The military service law of the Federal Republic of Germany states specifically that "whoever is opposed on grounds of conscience to participation in *every use of weapons between states* and therefore refuses active military duty with weapons may perform, in place of military duty, a civilian alternative service outside the Federal defense force." Reference to the specific case of the "use of weapons between states" makes it possible, even necessary, to separate the issue of objection to wars "between states" from other instances of resort to violence. Such phrasing would help to forestall the practice of employing absolute rejection of all uses of violence as the effective criterion of eligibility for conscientious objector status.[5]

The legal provisions for conscientious objection under existing United States law are based upon the premise that only those who completely and totally reject the use of war should be given alternative kinds of service. These provisions do not care for those who regard a particular war as unjust while still holding to a belief that under some circumstances war can be a legitimate instrument of national policy. But the position of an individual in the latter category has had, as we have seen, as long and fully as honorable a standing in Christian teaching as has opposition to all wars.

When the present draft law was considered in the spring of 1967 there was a brief flurry of discussion about the possibility of providing for conscientious objection to particular war. A presidentially appointed Advisory Commission on Selective Service had before it two proposals for modifying the ways of defining and dealing with conscientious objection. One proposal started from the premise that the duty (not merely the right!) to object to a particular war on moral grounds has an even greater significance in the religious heritage of the Western world than does a sectarian objection to all wars. It suggested that the present requirement of absolute pacifism be stricken from the law and that in its stead a young man be required to defend his objection to war, whether in terms of all wars or some wars, before a competent panel charged to determine his sincerity (but not his "correctness" on the moral or policy question). This procedure was believed to have distinct advantages for the moral tone of the nation because "young men would be required to reflect on the issues of war and peace, under the guidance of their mentors, and thus [be] enabled properly to form their consciences at an early age."[6]

The second proposal felt that the issues should be dealt with in the following manner:

First, the provisions of the present law should be retained for the absolute pacifist. Second, those whose objection is not against war in all forms, but against a particular conflict, should be given a more narrow option. They should be excused from combatant service, but they should be required to serve in a noncombatant military capacity, under conditions of hardship and even of hazard, and perhaps for a

107

longer period (for example, 3 years). This latter option should be liberally conceded to those who elect it, but without the requirement that they show affirmative proof that their objection to combatant service is on properly moral grounds.[7]

The proposal to extend the provisions of the Selective Service Act to permit conscientious objection to particular wars raises complex problems that a mature society ought to face fairly and realistically. But witnesses who appeared before the House Armed Services Committee on May 5, 1967, to testify on the subject do not seem to have been heard with a willing openness to explore the issues. A representative from the Methodist Board of Christian Social Concerns was asked (or told) in the course of the exchange: "There are only two ideologies in the world. One is represented by Jesus Christ and the other by the hammer and sickle. Which do you prefer?" Another witness, from a Quaker group, was asked, "Are you now or have you even been a member of the Communist party of the United States?"[8]

Such short shrift for a venturesome idea is not too surprising. Congress often trails behind the moral outlook of thoughtful segments of the society. What is more discouraging is to find otherwise informed and sensitive men caricaturing the suggestion. In an advertisement that appeared in *The New York Times* under the sponsorship of Freedom House, Inc., the following proposition was set over several prominent signatures:

[Our people, including the critics of the Vietnam war, should reject as a fantasy the proposition] *that military service in this country's armed forces is an option exercisable solely at the discretion of the indi-*

vidual. No nation anywhere, now or in the past, has ever recognized that principle. Those who urge individual defiance on moral grounds merely betray the genuine tenets of conscientious objection which our people respect.[9]

Tucked in with several others, this statement was designed to question the manner in which protests against the war in Vietnam were being conducted. It may have been aimed at direct violations of the draft law such as filing of admittedly false claims for conscientious objection as a means of evading service. Still, it was unfortunate because it gave support to the feeling that selective objection is by its very nature whimsical, careless, and shallow.

More genuine difficulties were cited in a majority report from the same Commission whose minority had advanced the two proposals for allowing for objection to specific wars. The majority, in voting to suggest retention of the requirement that conscientious objection be based upon opposition to all forms of war, noted five considerations: First, they felt that there is too much difficulty in finding agreement about Christian teaching in situations where men draw distinctions between different wars. Secondly, they maintained that any minority opposed to a particular war should express its concerns through normal political channels and claim no exemption from the consequences of a majority decision. Thirdly, that selective objection to war might open the doors to selective objection to other laws and tear down the fabric of government. Fourthly, the majority of the Commission felt that it was morally dubious (presumably as proposed in the second alternative) to permit a selective pacifist to avoid combat in

109

a war he regards as unjust yet to perform noncombatant service in its support. Lastly, they declared that "a determination of the justness or unjustness of any war could only be made within the context of that war itself," and that to open the door for men in the Armed Forces to make such judgments would have a disastrous effect upon the morale of the Armed Forces.[10]

Significant extensions of freedom are not easily legislated especially under the duress of war and when the supporters of such ideas are disorganized and largely inarticulate. Fresh ideas must be seeded, incubated, and then nourished to fruition by sustained advocacy. Often it requires crisis conditions to dramatize the existence of a problem and martyrs to make visible the injustices and difficulties in the *status quo*.

Support for the right of objection to particular wars has not been without advocacy. In May, 1966, the 178th General Assembly of The United Presbyterian Church U.S.A. urged Congress "to examine new proposals for universal service to the end that those who cannot conscientiously serve in a particular war may give alternative service to the nation," but the subsequent General Assembly flinched in its support. In February, 1967, the General Board of the National Council of Churches adopted a policy statement recommending the extension of present provisions for conscientious objection to include "those who are conscientiously opposed to a particular war." In the summer of 1967 the General Synod of the United Church of Christ went on record in favor of the same provisions.

Roger Shinn made a careful presentation before the Senate Armed Services Committee urging favor-

able consideration for some provisions in the law to
deal with the selective objector. He took account of
some of the objections to the proposal, avoided specifying any precise ways to implement it, and stressed the
importance of the matter in relationship to our heritage
of freedom:

> The proposal we offer would make a real difference
> to our society, even to our national honor. We would
> be saying to ourselves and to the world . . . "This is
> the kind of people we are—a people who believe in
> freedom of conscience even when it is inconvenient."

> Societies are stronger, although not always more com-
> fortable, if they keep alive the right of conscientious
> dissent. The difficulties they agree to accept in the
> process are the evidence of their devotion to free-
> dom.[11]

Ralph Potter has suggested that those seriously
committed to the extension of the provisions for conscientious objection must spell out more clearly than
they have yet been able to do the criteria by which ex-
emptions might be claimed. They should suggest procedures for measuring the sincerity of conscience if
the present administrative test of objection to all violence (which is not truly a test of sincerity) is rendered
irrelevant. Many of the more reasonable opponents of
selective objection might be persuaded to change their
minds if they could see how such a system would work.

Some countries seem to have succeeded with ways
of treating conscience that are much more liberal than
the present American pattern. In the midst of the last
war, with passions running high, Britain exempted
some men whose opposition to the war was selective.[12]
"The Scandinavian countries (Denmark, Sweden,

Norway and Finland) grant conscientious objector status to anyone who as proof of sincerity will serve alternative civilian service for a longer time than is required for military duty."[13]

Although there may be administrative problems, the main obstacle to American recognition of the right of conscience to object to a specific war is probably that strand of bellicose patriotism which looks upon military service as the only significant contribution to the national welfare. All thoughtful men, even though divided on the moral issue of war in general and Vietnam in particular, can help to cultivate a new climate in which various sacrificial contributions to the tremendous social needs of our nation and the world would be accorded equal acceptance.

CONSCIENCE AND THE USES OF CIVIL DISOBEDIENCE

Even the most enlightened nations can fail to make the provisions of their laws sufficiently broad to care for all cases of conscientious objection to war. Moreover, there is always the possibility that rigid and arbitrary administrative practices will deny the relief intended by the law in the case of a particular individual. Under such circumstances the truly conscientious objector has little choice but "to obey God rather than man." This choice is the final refuge of the conscience.

Disobedience of the law can also be a political device designed to embarrass or to disrupt the functionings of society. When so used, either as a means of witness against, or as an instrument of resistance to, existing policy, its moral meaning is entirely different. Civil disobedience of this sort should be understood as a form of power, is basically "militant," and is likely to elicit very different responses from public opinion and existing authority.

The first of these uses, involving acceptance of punishment for refusal to obey an order that is contrary to conscience, may not even be a case of "civil disobedience." The obedience to the state remains, but expresses itself as willingness to accept the penalties of the law rather than to violate the dictates of conscience. All the structures of constituted authority remain acknowledged. There is no attempt at escape or subversion. Indeed, actions taken on these grounds can become the means for instigating one of the impressive lawful processes of civilization—judicial review of the constitutionality of legislation and of administrative fairness in its enforcement.

Civil disobedience to a lawful order is a precondition for taking the case of an aggrieved conscience before the courts. It might be used, for example, to extend and modify provisions for conscientious objection to include the selective objector. What seems presently impossible to attain through legislative process might come about by judicial review. The 1948 Selective Service Act was modified to cover nontheistic objection by such a process, though in the Seeger case the Supreme Court dodged the constitutional issue by reaching a ruling based upon administrative considerations.

The constitutional issue in the case of selective objection centers around the fact that the exemption for those who are religiously opposed to all wars favors one religious position and excludes an equally religious one. It is no more religious to object to all wars on grounds of conscience than to object to a particular war on the same grounds. Since Congress is enjoined from passing legislation that favors one religion over another, the present law may plausibly be considered unconstitutional.

We do not know whether the Supreme Court would agree to review a case of professed objection to a particular war. It cannot be required to do so. To test this issue would require the most careful planning. It would entail finding an individual of impeccable character and unquestioned religious sincerity who is not deferrable on other grounds and whose opposition to but one particular war is well articulated. He would need to apply for exemption as a conscientious objector, filling out the questionnaire with sufficient care to center the issue on selective refusal. He would need to have his claim denied by the authorities for the specific reason in question, exhaust all appeal and administrative procedures, and finally take his case to court with the full realization that he might lose the whole process and have to spend time in jail or else admit his insincerity.

In similar cases, arising from men already in uniform who have developed doubts about the moral legitimacy of war after entering service, the Court has consistently refused to accept appeals. The Court seems to respect a long-established precedent for permitting executive decisions during wartime to stand even when there are genuine and pressing problems of legality involved. Fred P. Graham has bluntly warned:

This tradition underscores the regrettable fact that wars are exercises of power, not law. In the jargon of the courts, questions about the conduct of wars tend not to be "justiciable"—susceptible to resolution in the courts—and nobody seriously expects the Supreme Court to resolve them.[14]

The Court's refusal to hear cases of conscientious objection to particular war from military personnel does not necessarily mean that it will refuse to hear such cases from civilians.

Military personnel do not escape the problems that involve possible disobedience for the sake of conscience. Our Government has given its official support to the proposition that individuals are responsible for wartime actions that violate standards of humane behavior. As a party to the war crime trials at Nuremberg it has endorsed in principle the Charter by which Nazi war criminals were brought to justice. Article 8 of that Charter declares, "The fact that the Defendant acted pursuant to order of his Government or of a superior shall not free him from responsibility, but may be considered in mitigation of punishment if the Tribunal determines that justice so requires."

An Army field manual published in 1956 put together sections from the Uniform Code of Military Justice, United States laws, and treaty obligations to guide the soldier on the law of land warfare. Among the practices listed as war crimes are: making use of poisoned or otherwise forbidden arms; treacherous request for quarter; maltreatment of dead bodies; firing on localities that are undefended and without military significance; poisoning of wells or streams; pillage or purposeless destruction; killing without trial spies or

115

other persons who have committed hostile actions. A soldier ordered to do any of these acts is obliged to resist his orders or else become a war criminal.[15]

While it is easy to specify such crimes abstractly, in the concrete situations of military duty it is difficult to be sure whether or not an order is unjust. Moreover, the soldier is more impressed with the obligation to obey his orders than with the responsibility to weigh and evaluate their moral legitimacy. Soldiers in modern guerrilla wars know of repeated incidents that border on violations of morally defensible practice and of international law. They shrug these off as part of the dirty business of war under modern conditions. When three enlisted men were brought to trial for shooting a defenseless war prisoner in Vietnam, *The New York Times* reported that other members of the same platoon "appeared quite startled that the murder of a prisoner of war whose hands are bound behind his back could be a war crime."[16] While such trials are rare, and generally do not decisively determine that the punishable actions were done under superior orders, it often turns out that enlisted men involved are punished and officers who may have given the orders are acquitted.

Moreover, the man in service may very well have heard of Captain Howard Brett Levy, a medical officer who refused to train Green Berets for duty which he deemed at odds with the standards enunciated in international laws. He was sentenced to three years at hard labor and dismissal from the service for willful disobedience of orders, seeking to promote disloyalty, and culpable negligence. Captain Levy appealed to the

Nuremberg principles and to medical ethics (which are presumably established on a more objective basis than a personal moral code) in his defense. His appeals to the courts have been unsuccessful.

The reluctance of military authorities to permit individuals to refuse orders on the grounds of conscience is easily understood. But how can we reasonably expect men of another country (after we have vanquished it) to stand trial as war criminals yet in our own Armed Forces refuse relief and judicial review to those who appeal to conscience in resisting unjust orders? Unless we carefully rethink these issues, we will find ourselves in a moral and legal quagmire of attitudes that are at best inconsistent and possibly hypocritical.

The moral issues raised by the use of civil disobedience as an instrument of social protest or of political power are very different from those which arise when civil disobedience is used as the last refuge of conscience. Civil disobedience that is employed to embarrass or to thwart the political processes of government is potentially disruptive. Even though the tactics are intended to be nonviolent, they amount to coercion and often interfere with the free exercise of conscience by others. Whatever the validity of conscience as a basis for refusing to obey orders that are morally unacceptable to the individual, appeals "above the law or to a higher law" to justify essentially coercive strategies become an entirely different matter.

Symbolic acts, such as the burning of draft cards in a public ceremony, probably stand somewhere between the category of refusal to violate one's own conscientious scruples and the use of civil disobedience as a social pressure. Such actions simply make vivid certain issues the public might otherwise ignore. They are more likely to be grating and annoying than a clear and present danger. Coercive actions, however, such as blocking the doors of induction centers or the access of fellow students to military information officers, move even farther along the spectrum.

William Robert Miller, writing months before the outbreak of resistant civil disobedience in the anti-Vietnam movement, and viewing these matters as a longtime and sympathetic student of nonviolence, seriously questioned the legitimacy of civil disobedience used as a tool of political coercion:

> Is it compatible with the spirit of nonviolence to run from the police, to use bodily force to break through a police cordon, to refuse to obey or resist arrest by physical noncooperation, compelling the police to push or carry the noncooperator? Such actions seem closer to the insurrectionary anarchism of Sorel and Bakunin than to anything envisaged by Thoreau, despite his talk of clogging the machinery of state. When such methods are invoked in the name of nonviolence without a context of broad popular sympathy as a cushion, the psychological repercussions can be very damaging. Gandhi advised great care and prudence to avoid inciting or needlessly antagonizing the authorities, and for the same reasons such acts can also alienate both moderate sympathizers and the neutral public or, given a revolutionary situation, undermine respect for lawful order in general and promote irresponsible, inflammatory responses leading to chaos. In the case of an isolated individual it may be written off as fanaticism, but when contemplated as part of a campaign, mass civil disobedience is dynamite.[17]

118

Those who would resort to civil disobedience as a protest against governmental policies may acknowledge all the dangers to which Miller points. But since they are not pacifists by persuasion, they do not look upon such problems with the same sense of moral difficulty as would a vocational pacifist. Many of the most active dissenters were raised upon the view that Christians will exercise power and influence in the political arena and accept the compromises that go with this responsibility. They have turned to civil disobedience out of frustration with the established processes of political decision, showing a courage and fortitude to engage in forms of protest that may lead to punishments even though as individuals many have not been directly liable to service in a conflict they consider unjust.

Opposition to war from peace movements has seldom stopped a nation from pursuing a military policy upon which it has embarked.[18] The logic of conflict and the power of war to perpetuate itself once a nation decides to use violence have usually been too strong for any minority, however determined, to reverse. Perhaps the nonpacifist opponents of a particular war will prove that an adamant minority can alter national policy if they have the requisite tenacity in dissenting from a national policy, but they may also escalate the quarrel into disruptions of social trust and order. Conscientious refusals to obey orders that violate the scruples of conscience, when attended by quiet acceptance of the punishments involved, place public officials in the posture of persecutors. On the other hand, when such officials resist coercive tactics that threaten the orderly conduct of government they appear to the public as defenders of a civil order that is

119

very dear. Under such circumstances public sentiment can lash back upon the dissenting minority. Those who turn to civil disobedience must bear in mind how such disobedience will affect the public welfare, lest in devotion to a single moral imperative they rend society apart.

But, if society is to remain resilient and healthy, great care must be exercised by public officials in meeting civil disobedience. They must not succumb to the temptation, whatever the public clamor, to give demonstrators the harsh stick of the law merely because "they have it coming to them." While officials cannot let a small group get its way simply because it musters the resolve to make an issue, neither should they develop a self-righteousness in defense of order that escalates into vindictive hostility. It is one thing to be firm; it is another to become fanatical.

Toward Mature and Fair Inclusion

War fires the passions to fever heat. Both those who believe that it is a necessary instrument of honorable survival and those who believe that it contradicts all humane morality hold their views with intense conviction. This deep conviction reflects the extent to which war is a problem of conscience. It can breed estrangement from, and distrust of, those who do not come to the same conclusions. Few divisions of opinion can disrupt human relationships more tragically than those involving morality and policy in times of conflict.

Opposition to war can no longer be dismissed as a freak minority opinion that can be discounted in

120

getting on with the business of church and state. If we have been able in the past to ignore problems raised by the presence of moral opposition to war, we can no longer do so in the future. The times call for a new set of responses, and the history of the period through which we are now passing may well be written in terms of how well we build constructive policies that recognize a radically disturbing division of dedicated opinion.

Any nation that can afford the luxury of unprecedented prosperity and affluence while conducting wars across the seas ought also to be able to broaden the freedom it can afford to give sincere conscience. If we can have guns and jets as well as bread, butter, and new appliances without limits, can we not also manage world responsibilities without driving young men from our land to escape the moral dilemmas that some of them sincerely feel to flow from living in this one? If the voluntary system works for allocating material resources to a limited war, why can't it be made to work for manpower? To develop a less coercive system than we have at present would be a small price to pay for providing a dedicated and highly motivated segment of our young people with a constructive alternative to protest, resistance, and withdrawal.

The church must come to recognize that its own spiritual health demands a frank acceptance of the plurality of conviction and witness that is within its fellowship. To the extent to which any church aims to be inclusive, whether as a local parish or as an ecumenical body, it must now take into account the range of conviction on the morality of war that is a present fact of the contemporary situation. Groups that are too

121

monolithic in their witness, whether as "peace churches" or as "supportive establishments," will forfeit that quality of inclusion which has traditionally been cherished by most Christians as a mark of the church. To maintain inclusiveness under contemporary conditions requires an embrace of diversity far greater than anything deliberately cultivated in the past.

For churches to take seriously the demand for inclusion under such conditions may require some self-accepted restraints. Those bodies which would identify the cause of Christ with the policy objectives of "hawks" must stop trumpeting their jingoistic wares with the implied sanction of the Almighty. "Doves" will also find themselves restrained from that self-righteous confidence which exudes so readily from the breasts of those who see themselves alone as the peace-making children of God. If this restraint does no more than bring an end to banal self-confidence about what is "moral" and what is "immoral" in particular statements made on religious grounds, it will significantly sober the atmosphere.

This is to plead for neither silence nor inaction. Obviously it is no service to God or to the cause of his church to sweep these issues under the rug. Woe to that church whose secretary told a visiting preacher, after a sermon on Vietnam: "I'm sorry you came! You got us all so upset!"[19] Rather, it is to plead for responsible discussion of these issues without obscuring their perplexity with excessively enthusiastic partisanship. Individuals should speak their pieces remembering that the counsels of religious men do not command credence simply because they are made in the name of faith. Voluntary associations gathered together for support of a particular point of view should speak out. They deserve to be attentively heard by other Christians, particularly to the extent to which their pronouncements are sober, thoughtful, informed, cogent, and judiciously fair. In order for the church to open its heart and mind to points of view on all sides, the points of view must be advocated!

The church should encourage dialogue on an informed level, engender creatively new thinking about the points of disagreement and divergence of moral judgment found among its members, and explore the alternatives that might be pursued. All of this requires that it should be at least as concerned with the tone and maturity of pronouncement on either side of the war/ peace issue as it is with the substantive judgments they represent. The trite, the cheap, the inflammatory, and the unreflective plea on either side of an issue are more to be condemned than any particular policy decision. Those who do their homework on problems of international affairs and who write about them with depth and perception deserve encouragement—not because they are "responsible" in the sense of supporting particular points of view but because they bring insights to tasks performed maturely. Those who advocate particular policies with emotive and passionate homilies should be called up short even if they may be "right" from a particular point of view. Merely to declare, without reference to historical criteria or canons of moral judgment, that a particular war is "unjust" exhibits a hortatory and declaratory judgment that can too easily be accepted or rejected rather than examined and debated. Such a procedure hardly improves upon

123

the unreflective and emotional support for war that has all too commonly come to be expected of Christian bodies that are enslaved by their culture.

Let us encourage our preachers to consider controversial issues of morality and of policy from the pulpit. Let them, in turn, acknowledge the right of hearers to hold their own convictions. Let us insist that our ministers of education treat these problems in church school and youth groups, lest we rear young men who reach eighteen (and their first draft questionnaire) without ever having been exposed to the issues. Let us encourage church boards, agencies, and assemblies to explore these matters, but to make pronouncements in such a way as not to insist by implication that Christians have but one mind about these questions.

Finally, we should give very special guidance to all members of the church concerning the cultivation of that candor and spiritual charity which enables men to live with one another despite disagreement. Those who decide they must conscientiously support or engage in armed conflicts must be expressly taught not to succumb either to hatred for an enemy abroad or to intolerance for those with whom they disagree at home. Those who find themselves unable to participate in war must be helped to overcome the spiritual temptations that affect individuals who find themselves cut off from those cultural enthusiasms and rituals which give a sense of belonging to the general community.

NOTES

CHAPTER I. THE CHANGING NATURE OF WAR

1. The text of the note containing this quotation is printed in *The New York Times,* September 23, 1937, p. 19. My attention to it was aroused by the careful discussion of the evolution of mass bombing found in Robert C. Batchelder, *The Irreversible Decision: 1939–1950* (Houghton Mifflin Company, 1962), pp. 170–189. My argument is dependent upon his analysis.

2. Batchelder, *op. cit.,* pp. 221 f.

3. Howard Schomer, "Christian Nonviolence in the Nuclear Age," in *Therefore Choose Life: Essays on the Nuclear Crisis* (London: The International Fellowship of Reconciliation, 1961), p. 21.

4. Helmut Gollwitzer, "Christian Commitment," in *ibid.,* p. 35.

5. *Pastoral Constitution of the Church in the Modern World,* Part II, Ch. Five, Sec. 80.

6. John C. Bennett, "Moral Urgencies in the Nuclear Context," in John C. Bennett (ed.), *Nuclear Weapons and the Conflict of Conscience* (Charles Scribner's Sons, 1962), p. 100.

7. See Herman Kahn, *On Thermonuclear War* (Princeton University Press, 1960); Kahn, *Thinking About the Unthinkable* (Horizon Press, 1962).

8. Paul Ramsey, *The Limits of Nuclear War: Thinking About the Do-able and the Un-do-able* (Council on Religion and International Affairs, 1963), p. 10.

9. Rutherford M. Poats, *Decision in Korea* (The McBride Company, 1954), p. xi.

10. Alfred Hassler, "Cops in Korea," in *Fellowship Magazine,* Vol. XVI, No. 8 (September, 1950), p. 5.

11. Robert T. Oliver, "The Periscope on Asia," September 2, 1949. Reprinted as a citation in *Verdict in Korea* (Bald Eagle Press, 1952), p. 207.

12. James Finn, editorial in *Worldview,* Vol. 9, No. 2 (February, 1966), p. 2.

CHAPTER II. Religious Support
for Conscientious Participation

1. Archbishop R. E. Lucey, in *The New York Times,* September 9, 1967, p. 16.

2. Augustine, *The City of God,* XIX. vii. Translation from Whitney J. Oates, *Basic Writings of Saint Augustine,* Vol. II (Random House, Inc., 1948), pp. 481 f.

3. Thomas Aquinas, *Summa Theologiae* II/II, Question XL.

4. Augustine, *Contra Faustum* I, XXII, Ch. 74. Thomas Aquinas cites this with approval in *Summa Theologiae* II/II, Question XL.

5. Pope Urban, quoted from Dana Carlton Munro, "Urban and the Crusaders" in *Translations and Reprints* (University of Pennsylvania Press, 1910), p. 4.

6. Decretals of Gratian, *Pars Secunda,* Causa XXIII, Question VIII, C. IX. Quoted in John Eppstein, *The Catholic Tradition of the Law of Nations* (London: Burns, Oates & Washbourne, Ltd., 1935), p. 82.

7. Ray H. Abrams, *Preachers Present Arms* (Round Table Press, 1933).

8. Henry Churchill King, "Grounds of Hope in the Present Crisis," in Frederick Lynch (ed.), *President Wilson and the Moral Aims of the War* (Fleming H. Revell Company, 1918), p. 71. In fairness to President King, it must be noted that he did warn against undue hatred of the enemy.

9. Billy Sunday, quoted in Abrams, *op. cit.,* p. 83.

10. James H. Maurer, "Has the Church Betrayed Labor?" in Jerome Davis (ed.), *Labor Speaks for Itself on Religion* (The Macmillan Company, 1929), p. 32.

11. Robert W. Tucker, *The Just War: A Study in Contemporary American Doctrine* (The Johns Hopkins Press, 1960); see especially Ch. I.

12. Robert E. Osgood, *Limited War: The Challenge to American Strategy* (The University of Chicago Press, 1957), p. 33.

13. Reinhold Niebuhr, editorial in *Christianity and Crisis,* February 10, 1941. Reprinted in D. B. Robertson (ed.), *Love and Justice* (The Westminster Press, 1957), p. 282.

14. Charles C. Morrison's editorials were collected, in revised form, in *The Christian and the War* (Willett, Clark & Company, 1942).

15. Roger L. Shinn, *Beyond This Darkness* (Association Press, 1946).

16. *Ibid.*, p. 55.

CHAPTER III. RELIGIOUS OPPOSITION TO PARTICIPATION IN WAR

1. Harry Emerson Fosdick, "My Account with the Unknown Soldier," in *The Christian Century*, Vol. LI, No. 23 (June 6, 1934), p. 756. Also the *Congressional Record*, Vol. 78, Part II (June 16, 1934), pp. 11971 f.

2. From an address, "Beyond Vietnam," given by Martin Luther King, Jr., in The Riverside Church, New York, April 4, 1967, under the auspices of Clergy and Laymen Concerned About Vietnam.

3. Tertullian, "The Chaplet" (or, "*De Corona*"), in A. Roberts and J. Donaldson (eds.), *The Ante-Nicene Fathers*, Vol. III (The Christian Literature Publishing Company, 1885), p. 99.

4. Burton Scott Easton (tr.), *The Apostolic Tradition of Hippolytus* (Cambridge: Cambridge University Press, 1934), p. 42.

5. Jean Lasserre, *War and the Gospel*, tr. by Oliver Coburn (Herald Press, 1962), p. 19.

6. David L. Dodge, "By Gospel Authority," in his *Autobiography*. This selection is taken from a portion reprinted in Peter Mayer (ed.), *The Pacifist Conscience* (Holt, Rinehart and Winston, Inc., 1966), p. 113.

7. G. H. C. MacGregor, *The New Testament Basis of Pacifism* (London: James Clarke & Company, 1936), pp. 16–34.

8. A. J. Muste, "Pacifism and Perfectionism," in Nat Hentoff (ed.), *The Essays of A. J. Muste* (The Bobbs-Merrill Company, Inc., 1967), p. 320.

9. Guy Franklin Hershberger, *War, Peace, and Nonresistance* (Herald Press, 1944), p. 225.

10. Devere Allen (ed.), *Pacifism in the Modern World*

(Doubleday & Company, Inc., 1929), p. xvi.

11. William Ellery Channing, *Discourses on War* (Ginn and Company, 1903), p. 2.

12. Adin Ballou, *Christian Non-Resistance, In All Its Important Bearings, Illustrated and Defended* (J. Miller M'Kim, 1846), p. 11.

13. William Lloyd Garrison, quoted in *New England Non-Resistance Society: Declaration of Principles,* 1838, from Mayer (ed.), *op. cit.,* pp. 126 f.

14. Thomas Merton, Preface to P. R. Régamey, *Non-violence and the Christian Conscience* (London: Darton, Longman & Todd, Ltd., 1966), p. 14.

15. Richard B. Gregg, *The Power of Non-violence* (J. B. Lippincott Company, 1934), p. 121.

16. Vera Brittain, *Humiliation with Honour* (Fellowship Publications, 1943), p. 47.

17. Henry David Thoreau, "Civil Disobedience," in *Miscellanies* (Houghton Mifflin Company, 1894), p. 142.

18. *Ibid.,* pp. 145 f.

19. Alan W. Watts, *This Is It and Other Essays on Zen and Spiritual Experience* (Pantheon Books, Inc., 1958), pp. 89 f.

20. Lao-tzu, *Tao and Wu Wei: A New Translation,* tr. by Bhikshu Wai-Tao and Dwight Goddard (Dwight Goddard, 1935), p. 44.

CHAPTER IV. MORALS AND POLICY

1. Paul Ramsey, "The Ethics of Intervention," in *The Review of Politics,* Vol. 27, No. 3 (July, 1965), p. 291.

2. *Ibid.,* p. 298.

3. Reinhold Niebuhr, "The Christian Faith and the World Crisis," in *Christianity and Crisis,* Vol. I, No. 1 (February 10, 1941). Also in D. B. Robertson (ed.), *Love and Justice* (The Westminster Press, 1957), p. 283.

4. Ramsey, "The Ethics of Intervention," *loc. cit.,* p. 293.

5. James V. Schall, "Wars Will Cease When . . .," in *Worldview,* Vol. 10, No. 5 (May, 1967), p. 10.

6. Robert A. Gessert, "Wars of National Liberation:

II," in *Worldview,* Vol. 9, No. 3 (March, 1966), pp. 4 f.

7. Manfred Halpern, *The Morality and Politics of Intervention* (Council on Religion and International Affairs, 1963), p. 33.

8. Quentin Quade, "Religion, Moral Authority, and Intervention," in *Worldview,* Vol. 9, No. 12 (December, 1966), p. 13.

9. Peter J. Riga, "An Open Letter: The American Catholic Bishop's Statement," in *Worldview,* Vol. 9, No. 12 (December, 1966), p. 7.

10. Samuel H. Magill, "Religion, Peace, and the Realists," a book review in *Worldview,* Vol. 10, No. 5 (May, 1967), pp. 14 f.

11. John C. Bennett, "From Supporter of War in 1941 to Critic in 1966," in *Christianity and Crisis,* Vol. XXVI, No. 2 (February 21, 1966), p. 13.

12. *Ibid.,* p. 14.

13. Editorial in *Christianity and Crisis,* Vol. XXVI, No. 3 (March 7, 1966), p. 1.

14. Robert McAfee Brown, Abraham J. Heschel, and Michael Novak, *Vietnam: Crisis of Conscience* (published simultaneously by Association Press, Behrman House, Herder & Herder, Inc., 1967).

15. *The New York Times,* May 6, 1967, p. 1.

16. See *The New York Times,* September 17, 1967, p. 16.

17. *Ibid.,* December 12, 1967, p. 15.

18. *Ibid.,* December 11, 1967, p. 13.

19. Howard Schomer, "An American Christian Looks at the Changing Communist World," in *Information Service,* Vol. XLVI, No. 16 (October 28, 1967), p. 1.

20. Halpern, *op. cit.,* p. 14.

21. See Charles West, "Christian Responsibility in Vietnam," in *Worldview,* Vol. 10, No. 5 (May, 1967).

CHAPTER V. THE STATE, THE CHURCH, AND CONSCIENCE

1. Quoted in David E. Roberts, "The Case of the Union Students," in *The Christian Century,* Vol. LVII, No.

44 (October 30, 1940), p. 1342.

2. *The New York Times,* November 22, 1967, p. 3.

3. *U.S. v. Seeger,* 380 U.S. 163 (1965), at 176 (p. 7).

4. *Annett v. U.S.,* 205 F2d 689 (10th Cir. 1953) at 691.

5. Ralph B. Potter, "Conscientious Objection to Particular Wars," in Donald A. Giannella (ed.), *Religion and the Public Order.* This quotation taken from a privately circulated, prepublication manuscript.

6. *In Pursuit of Equity: Who Serves When Not All Serve?* (Report of The National Advisory Commission on Selective Service, U.S. Government Printing Office, 1967), p. 49.

7. *Ibid.,* p. 50.

8. *The New York Times,* May 6, 1967, p. 6.

9. *Ibid.,* November 30, 1966, p. 37.

10. *In Pursuit of Equity,* pp. 50 f.

11. Roger L. Shinn, *Testimony on Selective Conscientious Objection,* April 14, 1967, Senate Armed Services Committee. (Reprinted in pamphlet form by the Council for Christian Social Action, United Church of Christ, 289 Park Avenue South, New York, N.Y., 10010.)

12. See Letter to the Editor by Fenner Brockway (Lord Brockway) in *The New York Times,* April 7, 1966, p. 38.

13. Jean Carper, *Bitter Greetings: The Scandal of the Military Draft* (Grossman Publishers, Inc., 1967), p. 142.

14. Fred P. Graham, quoted in *The New York Times,* November 12, 1967, p. 12 E.

15. United States Army field manual FM 27-10, *The Law of Land Warfare* (July, 1956), p. 180.

16. *The New York Times,* August 6, 1967, Sec. 4, p. 2.

17. William Robert Miller, *Nonviolence: A Christian Interpretation* (Association Press, 1964), p. 80.

18. I take this to be a conclusion indicated by Kenneth E. Boulding in his book *Conflict and Defense: A General Theory* (Harper & Row, Publishers, Inc., 1962), pp. 333 f.

19. See *The Christian Century,* Vol. LXXXV, No. 1 (January 3, 1968), p. 14.